ART & DESIGN

R40136

EDITORIAL OFFICES:
42 LEINSTER GARDENS, LONDON W2 3AN
TEL: 071-402 2141 FAX: 071-723 9540

HOUSE EDITOR: Nicola Hodges
EDITORIAL TEAM: Iona Spens,
Katherine MacInnes, Ramona Khambatta
ART EDITOR: Andrea Bettella
CHIEF DESIGNER: Mario Bettella
DESIGNER: Jan Richter

SUBSCRIPTION OFFICES:
UK: VCH PUBLISHERS (UK) LTD
8 WELLINGTON COURT, WELLINGTON STREET
CAMBRIDGE CB1 1HZ
TEL: (0223) 321111 FAX: (0223) 313321

USA AND CANADA: VCH PUBLISHERS INC
303 NW 12TH AVENUE DEERFIELD BEACH,
FLORIDA 33442-1788 USA
TEL: (305) 428-5566 / (800) 367-8249
FAX: (305) 428-8201

ALL OTHER COUNTRIES:
VCH VERLAGSGESELLSCHAFT MBH
BOSCHSTRASSE 12, POSTFACH 101161
69451 WEINHEIM
FEDERAL REPUBLIC OF GERMANY
TEL: 06201 606 148 FAX: 06201 606 184

D1612555

CONTENTS

ART & DESIGN **MAGAZINE**

*Deutsche Romantic • Yves Klein • Shirazeh
Houshiary • Boyd Webb • Helen Sear • Manhole Covers • Books • Academy Highlights*

ART & DESIGN **PROFILE** No 40

THE CONTEMPORARY SUBLIME

Yves Klein, Ohne Titel, *1957*

Caspar David Friedrich,
Solitary Tree, *1822*

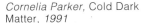

Cornelia Parker, Cold Dark
Matter, *1991*

DEUTSCHE ROMANTIC

THE POET AS ARTIST
Rosemary Ashton

Extracts from a lecture on the emergence in late 18th and early 19th-century Britain and Germany of 'Romantic' ideas about the nature of the artist, particularly the poet, delivered at the Goethe Institute, London in connection with the South Bank Festival of German Romanticism.

Certain topics of critical interest arose in both England (and Scotland) and Germany in the later 18th century; for example, questions about the nature of poetry, the poet, and the faculty of Imagination (often written, for emphasis, within the period with a capital 'I'). What is the origin of poetic activity? What is the relation of the subject to the object in perception and, by extension, in imaginative creation? In particular, what is the relation of the poet to external nature (well known to be the chief interest of Wordsworth in his great poem *The Prelude*)? A stress was now put on the 'organic unity' of a work of art, and the power and genius of the artist was the object of attention. This represents a perceptible shift from the traditional emphases of the previous 'neo-classical' generation on questions of taste, judgment, decorum, and the moral value of literature.

It is not that such interests disappear in the Romantic period, but a shift of emphasis puts the stress on psychological and aesthetic, rather than moral, questions in relation to art. Indeed it was Coleridge who introduced our modern sense of the word 'aesthetic' – namely having to do with the art of criticism – into English in a letter published in *Blackwood's Magazine* in 1821. The German writer Baumgarten had first used the word in this sense in his work *Aesthetica*, published as early as the 1750s. This is but one of many ways in which German notions fed into English culture, and it is significant that the conduit was Coleridge.

In keeping with the new interest in psychological matters, much of the subject matter of English and German Romantic literature concerns the artist as hero. One thinks of Goethe's phenomenally successful work – translated into several languages and a terrific success throughout Europe – *The Sorrows of Young Werter* (1774), which spawned a host of imitators, as well as a craze for Werter costumes, Werter china and Werter eau-de-cologne, and Werter-like suicide among the young men of

Europe; or of *The Prelude*, which was subtitled 'The Growth of a Poet's Mind'.

It is not too much to say that an intellectual climate emerged in which the poet was, in poetry and in critical theory, the object of his own scrutiny. This is true of Schiller, the brothers Schlegel, ETA Hoffmann and others in Germany, and of Coleridge, Wordsworth, Keats and Shelley in England.

About the middle of the 18th century a movement arose in Germany in response to the long political and cultural hegemony, or yoke, as it was felt to be, of France. Germany was not even a political entity, but a heterogeneous bunch of petty principalities, which did not even share a common language. Frederick the Great of Prussia is well known for refusing to speak the 'barbaric' German tongue at his court, preferring French, the language of polite society and polite literature. Writers and critics such as Lessing and Herder began the cultural revolt. In their essays on literature and culture, they fought to free German language and literature from the foreign yoke. The battle was fought on two fronts: firstly, a literature should be truly national, indigenous, original, not dependent on foreign rules and examples (here the neo-classical unities as applied to drama, with Racine and Corneille as models, were chiefly in mind); secondly, since Germans had more in common with the British than with the French in terms of their language and, especially according to Herder, their northern climate and culture, they should look to England, a country rich in original literature, for inspiration.

There was, of course, a contradiction here – though a fruitful one – for these German writers were calling on would-be German poets at once to be original, to throw off imitation of the French, and yet to imitate another model, the English one. But with some ingenuity they solved the paradox. They concentrated on one English author as a desirable model, Shakespeare. And the point they made about Shakespeare was that he had freed himself from the dramatic unities; he was a great 'natural' genius, a 'Prometheus', a force of nature. In the flow of their adoring rhetoric, Shakespeare and Nature became synonymous and as such the model for striving German poets.

Both Herder and Goethe wrote rhapsodic

FROM ABOVE: Philipp Otto Runge, Self Portrait, 1801; Henri Fuseli, The Nightmare, 1781; Caspar David Friedrich, Mist in the Elbe Valley, 1821, from The Romantic Spirit in German Art 1790-1990, Hayward Gallery, London

essays on Shakespeare along these lines in the 1770s. And Goethe answered his own call in his historical drama, clearly prompted by the example of Shakespeare's histories, *Gotz von Berlichingen* (1773), as did Schiller in his *Sturm und Drang* tragedy of the good and bad brothers (drawing shamelessly on Edgar and Edmund in *King Lear*), *The Robbers* (1781). The young Coleridge read this play in translation in 1794 when his head was full of his new friend Robert Southey and their Utopian plan to set up a Pantisocracy on the banks of the Susqehanna, and he dashed off a letter after midnight, asking, 'My God, Southey, who is this Schiller, this convulser of the heart?' and sending his friend a rhapsodic sonnet he had scribbled 'To the Author of "The Robbers"'.

> Schiller! that hour I would have wish'd to die
> If thro' the shuddering midnight I had sent
> That fearful voice, a famish'd Father's cry –
> Lest in some after moment aught more mean
> Might stamp me mortal! A triumphant shout
> Black Horror scream'd, and all her goblin rout
> Diminish'd shrunk from the more withering scene!
> Ah! Bard tremendous in sublimity!
> Could I behold thee in thy loftier mood
> Wandering at eve with finely-frenzied eye
> Beneath some vast old tempest-swinging wood!
> Awhile with mute awe gazing I would brood:
> Then weep aloud in a wild ecstasy

Coleridge, To the Author of the Robbers *1794*

Note the phrase 'finely-frenzied eye'; it is an appropriate echo of Theseus's line in Act V of *A Midsummer Night's Dream* about 'the poet's eye, in a fine frenzy rolling'. Coleridge chooses it as a proper tribute to Schiller's genius, and perhaps also as an acknowledgment of the visible Shakespearean influence on Schiller.

Next most important to Shakespeare in this programme for the revival of German literature was the ballad literature of Germany. Encouraged by Bishop Percy's recent collection of English ballads, *Reliques of Ancient English Poetry* (1765), Germans sought out old German ballads, and – as had happened with Macpherson's so-called 'discovery' and translation of an early Scottish epic by the bard 'Ossian', a success in Germany as well as in Britain – where they could not find original ballads they composed their own. August Burger's Gothic ballad of a ghostly ride by night, *Lenore*, loosely based on a Scottish ballad, 'Sweet William's Ghost', was the most celebrated of these. It offers a single example of how an influence could begin in Britain, with Percy and 'Ossian', inspire activity in Germany, and travel back to Britain to have some literary success there. *Lenore* was translated in the 1790s by several Britons, including the Poet

Laureate, HJ Pye; one JT Stanley, whose translation was illustrated by Blake; and the young Walter Scott.

But, important though Scott is in any story of the influence of German literature in Britain, there is one writer whose relationship with Germany was in every way more significant, though also fraught with complexities. This was, of course, Coleridge, who read widely in the literature, criticism, and philosophy of Germany, and who, inasmuch as he came to be the representative critic (as well as poet) of English Romanticism, injected that Romanticism with much that was German in origin.

Coleridge asked the famous question in *Biographia Literaria*, 'What is poetry?' and, in a manner which illustrates what we may call the 'Romantic Revolution' in aesthetics, answered it as follows:

> What is poetry? Is so nearly the same question with, what is a poet? that the answer to the one is involved in the solution of the other. For it is a distinction resulting from the poetic genius itself, which sustains and modifies the images, thoughts, and emotions of the poet's own mind. The poet, described in ideal perfection, brings the whole world of man into activity, with the subordination of its faculties to each other, according to their relative worth and dignity. He diffuses a tone and spirit of unity, that blends, and (as it were) fuses, each into each, by that synthetic and magical power, to which we have exclusively appropriated the name of imagination.

Biographia Literaria, Coleridge, 1817, Ch 14

Shakespeare was the great example of the imaginative poet. Herder had used him as propaganda for a new German literature. The very German dramas and poems which resulted from Herder's 'call to arms' travelled back to England to fill a gap – there was a notable dearth of original drama in England in the period – and to energise British writers. This is true of the Gothic genre both in its glories, among which must be counted 'The Ancient Mariner' as well as Mary Shelley's *Frankenstein*, and its absurdities and excesses, such as Matthew Lewis's notorious novel *The Monk*.

The extraordinary literary and philosophical Renaissance in Germany in the later 18th century could not itself have taken just the form it did without the reception, absorption, and imitation of British theory and practice, whether in the thoughts of Burke on the sublime and Hume and Hartley on the theory of association or in the ballads collected by Percy and the plays of the divine Shakespeare.

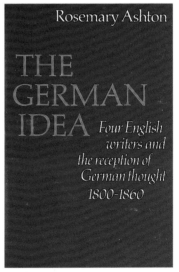

The German Idea, (HB) Cambridge University Press 1980, (PB) Libris 1994. Rosemary Ashton is Professor of English at University College London

IV

YVES KLEIN

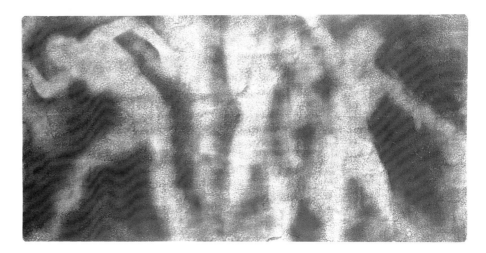

Yves Klein is often identified as the artist who ceaselessly used the colour ultramarine blue (which he named 'IKB' International Klein Blue). His adoption of blue and the monochrome aesthetic was a way to remove expressionistic, representational, compositional and personalising elements from his art. It was, moreover, a way to focus on open expanses of space, thereby encouraging the discovery of the evocative, poetic power of colour and the sensorial spectacle of colour as space. Monochrome blue signified the indefinable and immateriality. IKB was designed as a means of awakening an individual's receptivity and liberating the senses.

Klein was not an artist who focused his concerns on craft or technique. His radicality also had nothing to do with developing a new 'style' or advocating a different kind of subject matter. Although he was clearly attentive to the appearance of the art object and preoccupied with inventive art-making procedures – as well as conceptual, performance, publicity, and thematic issues – none of these factors were ends in, and of, themselves. On the contrary, they were all means that were variously used to augment the art experience.

Like many other great artists of the 20th century, Klein did more than create extraordinary works of art: he challenged the very idea of what art was, is, and might be. Indeed, his rebellion was against a fixed premise that might circumscribe the art work or imprison it in any one classifying definition. Klein typically did not conceive of his art objects as isolated entities. To accentuate the relationship between the work, its surroundings, and viewers, he developed evocative modes of display and theatrical, highly unconventional, process-oriented events.
Hayward Gallery London, Feb-April, 1995, Museo Nacional Centro de Arte Reina Sofia, Madrid, May-August 1995

OPPOSITE: Anthropométrie, *1960; FROM ABOVE:* Hiroshima, *1991;* Ohne Titel, *1961*

SHIRAZEH HOUSHIARY

Shirazeh Houshiary has become increasingly involved with a mathematical understanding of form. She uses a precise, but not empirical approach in an attempt to comprehend the multiplicity of the world. Through assigning symbolic expression to her Sufi beliefs, Houshiary has developed a spiritual approach to her work. Sufism, in philosophical terms, concerns itself with a discussion of the reality of existence. As a religion it is concerned with creating a way in which the unity of the physical and spiritual worlds and all that they contain may be recognised. Within Sufi thought, as in many other traditions, it is believed that three movements make up the creation of the universe: ascent, descent and expansion. At the centre of this universe is the point of knowledge in a state of purity around which move all forms of existence.

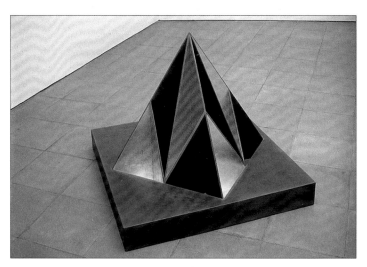

The content of the works is not simply cerebral, however, but provokes a powerful sense of physical interaction. The participation of the viewer is essential and the evocation of sound and movement contributes to a very real experience. In the sculpture *Threeness*, square lead boxes are placed on the floor to form a triangle. With the first element, an internal experience is suggested by the image of a complex ebb-like form which descends towards the base of the square. In the second part, the form expands outwards into a pyramid in which the lead is transformed into gold as it reaches upwards. In the third, floating on the surface of the lead is placed a small copper triangle which is intensified by the luminosity of the metal – thus manifesting the three movements of descent, ascent and expansion respectively in each of its elements, *Threeness* expresses a sense of unity.

The Way to the Unseen is another three-part work which begins with a large lead cube at the centre of which is a cube of silver surrounded by a series of squares the geometry of which implies a rotating motion. In the second part, the lead weight of the containing form is removed to reveal the core of squares and finally in the third section this complex form itself is removed to leave a double cube of reflected light.

Lisson Gallery, London, Sept-Oct 1994

FROM ABOVE: Threeness, *1984, lead, copper and gold leaf;* The Way to the Unseen, *1994, lead and platinum leaf*

BOYD WEBB

Boyd Webb's work is perhaps best described as the 'black comedy of procreation'. He is concerned with cycles and signs of life and death in a way that engages with the political reality of Western fertility rates and the epoch of AIDS. He uses symbols of reproduction to provide a controversial commentary on the disturbing biological desitiny of nature. However Webb's interest in Islamic 'Sufi' mysticism means that he tempers his warnings with wit. A disquieting juxtaposition is achieved by using attractive or recognisable objects in a narrative which often evokes less attractive or sinister associations.

The witty poetic and historic coincidence which is the basis of *Donor* is the fact that sheep's guts were used as the first 'natural' condom in western Europe. The transparent coils are a sheep's intestines but Webb transforms them into an ornate containment which holds and collects the simulated sperms.

Tutelar, 1993 is constituted of the yolk of an egg held by a human hand, in a string bag over a pile of sperm-shaped objects made out of plasticine which are racing towards the egg over a field of rough patterned wallpaper. Here, the polished presentation of familiar objects is set against the pathos of the Darwinian struggle of life-bearing and engendering forms.

None of the objects which comprise *Awe* are organic and yet, like Max Ernst and Yves Tanguy, Webb manages to evoke the all too legible terrain of the body's interior landscapes. His fascination with the erotics of material enables him to animate and transform unpromising everyday objects into disturbing compositions with which we are forced to identify.

Webb's work has been described as 'what Surrealism looks like when it has been diagnosed HIV-positive'. Indeed his tendency towards the biomorphic ironies of Surrealism is in the tradition of Salvador Dali whose tortuous mounds of indiscriminate flesh were executed in an admirable technique but were ultimately repulsive.

Orchard Gallery, Derry, Sept-Oct 1994

FROM ABOVE: Tutelar, *1993;* Awe, *1992;* Donor, *1994*

HELEN SEAR

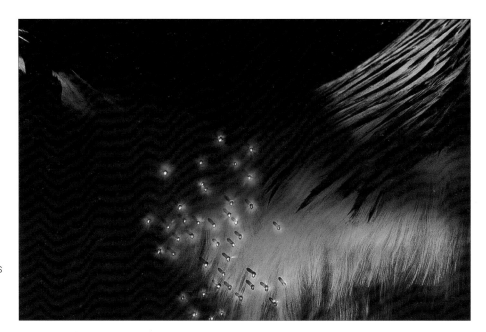

Helen Sear's work uses photographic and electronic media to make a link between landscape and the body, and all of the associated – mapping; health; surveillance – are alluded to in her work. The first space of the exhibition 'Gone to Earth' consists of a series of seven constructed photographs, unglazed, in dark heavy frames, which have the quality of night-time aerial photographs. They bring together half-glimpsed images of nocturnal creatures and an impression of landscape, often indicated by tiny lights reminiscent of cities at night. In the first 'linking' gallery space, images taken from brain scans are placed against a background setting. In another, a sleeping face is seen marked with the pen-marks of a surgical operation that is about to take place. In the corridor into the darkened room, lit only by the installation, two lightboxes together make a pair of eyes.

The room itself its like an apse, with the curved wall taking up its whole width at the far end. The installation consists of a panorama of dissolving ultrasound foetal scans which exaggerate the curved wall of the gallery. Three images can be seen simultaneously, taking up exactly the whole semi-circular curve of the wall. The central image is constantly changing through the use of a dissolve unit. The images themselves are scans that were found, and are therefore covered in scratches. In front of this drama, suspended horizontally in space, is a transparent sheet into which is inserted a series of LEDs, mapping the frontal acupuncture points of a male figure and moving constantly in waves. The relationship between the earth, the body and physical and psychological well-being is thus complete. Because of the subject matter, one might imagine that the atmosphere of the space would be threatening (noctural creatures, brain scans, foetal scans), but the overwhelming impression is of peace, of a relationship between body awareness, our relationship to the earth, and our overall well-being.

John Hansard Gallery, Sept-November 1994
Images from the series 'Gone to Earth I-VIII'

MANHOLE COVERS
RICHARD GLOVER

Throughout inner London are numerous steel covers inserted into the pavement enabling access to essential utilities such as water, power and telecommunications. They are generally known as manhole covers.

Manhole covers service a simple function and would not normally be considered for their aesthetic value. The photographer Richard Glover maintains that they are, however, thoughtfully designed objects in their own right and graphic examples of the interrelationship of time and the vagaries of the environment.

The designs of the covers are generally simple but bold reflecting their utilitarian function. Some coal chute covers incorporate motifs that are almost ornate. Questions remain unanswered: who were the designers? What were their constraints, their influences?

'Through my photographs I want to arrest the attention of fellow pedestrians and present this quiet beauty which radiates at our feet.'
Barbican, London, October 1994

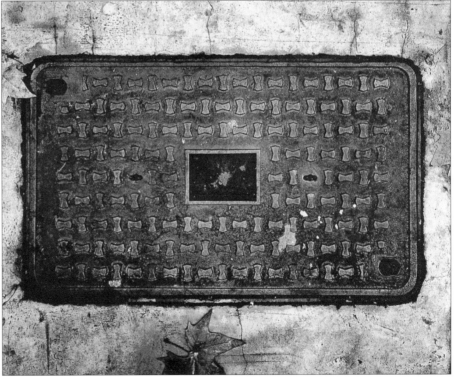

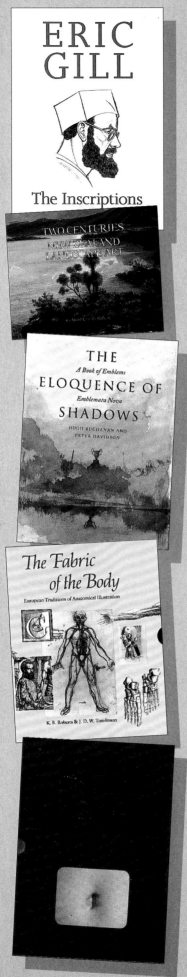

ERIC GILL The Inscriptions by David Peace, Herbert Press, b/w ills, 208 pp, HB £35

Eric Gill was one of the foremost artist-craftsmen of the 20th century, well known as a sculptor, engraver and polemicist, as well as a typeface designer. He has recently found renewed notoriety through revelations about his private life that are at odds with his image as the pious offspring of generations of clergymen. This book, however, considers only the carved stone inscriptions produced by Gill and his workshop in the years 1901-40. Nearly 1,000 of these have been documented by David Peace, himself a glass engraver with a passion for lettering, in a labour of love that has taken over 40 years and involved close collaboration with Gill's brother. Each inscription is recorded, the design briefly described and the most notable works asterisked. The catalogue raisonné includes appendices on Gill's work on war memorials, heraldry, medals and stamps, as well as a county-by-county guide to the whereabouts of all Gill's known lettering work. This will probably cause the reader to take a fresh look at familiar inscriptions, for this astonishingly prolific craftsman crops up in some unexpected corners.

TWO CENTURIES OF NEW ZEALAND LANDSCAPE ART by Roger Blackley, Auckland City Gallery, 127pp, colour ills, PB £N/A

Sydney Parkinson produced sepia landscape drawings on Captain James Cook's first visit to New Zealand. These and the watercolours William Hodges painted on the second trip mark the first 'European' response to that dramatic landscape. Cook believed that Hodges had 'delineated the face of the country with such judgement as will at once convey a better idea of it than can be expressed by words'. Hodges' 'Cascade Cove, Dusky Bay' 1775 translates New Zealand into the language of Edmund Burke's sublime: 'a lonely Maori family posed against gloomy forests, a vast cataract shimmering under a rainbow'. These landscapes are arranged in chronological order to give an idea of the changing attitudes towards them. Charles Heaphy's painting of Kauri Forest,

Wairoa River, Kaipara shows the potential for timber trading and his sketches were included in Edward Jerningham Wakefield's *Adventure in New Zealand*, a portfolio of pictorial propaganda intended to encourage colonisation. The last images consist of photographs of 'beach culture' – the landscape in relation to tourism and city scapes which provide a commentary on the effect of industry on the environment.

THE ELOQUENCE OF SHADOWS A Book of Emblems, Emblemata Nova by Hugh Buchanan and Peter Davidson, Thirdpart Publications, 32pp, colour ills, Collectors Edition £185/Standard Edition HB £32.50

The artist Hugh Buchanan and the poet Peter Davidson have collaborated to produce this book of emblems. Such books evolved during the Renaissance and were illustrated, each picture having its own motto and explanatory text. Work and image acted in tension with each other to provide matter for meditation or further thought. Hugh Buchanan argues that our retrospective perception of the picturesque is inaccurate. He claims that a 19th-century painting of a crumbling mill would have expressed poverty rather than the rural idyll. Buchanan deliberately chooses features of the 20th century such as pylons to communicate a reality and to encourage a reassessment of these and other icons of the modern age. The embracing of industrialism is not new: the Art Deco movement of the 1920s was based on it and LS Lowry made his living out of it – but Buchanan's collaboration with Davidson has produced a clever juxtaposition of 'living latin', provided by Father Hendrie, with the paintings to produce this emblem book: a visually satisfying and mentally thought provoking, ironic commentary on the age in which we live.

THE FABRIC OF THE BODY European Traditions of Anatomical Illustration KB Roberts & JDW Tomlinson, Oxford University Press, 638pp, b/w ills, HB £95

This is a survey and an anthology of the major developments, styles and trends in anatomical illustration from medieval times up to the

development of the camera. The interrelationship between art and anatomy can be seen in the images presented in this book which show that such technical illustrations can also have their own strange and unusual beauty. In the universities and academies of Renaissance Europe scholars and artists were preoccupied with anatomy and the discovery of human form by dissection. The 16th century saw the beginning of the scientific development of those studies with the private work of Leonardo da Vinci and the publication of the first illustrated printed anatomies. It was by illustration rather than text that anatomists and their illustrating artists, printers, and publishers spread information. These pictures reveal their attitudes towards the living and the dead.

THE BODY Photoworks of the Human Form by William A Ewing, Thames and Hudson, 430pp, b/w and colour ills, PB £16.95

This book studies the art of depicting human bodies through the medium of photography. This chronological record communicates volumes about the evolution of cultural perceptions of the body. The possibilities are endless: from the naked Zulu women photographed by T H Huxley and John Lamprey in 1860 according to their standard procedures for ethnological photography, through a medical fascination with deformity and 19th-century erotica, to the acrobatic nudes of Philip Trager and Lois Greenfield of the 1990s.

Most of the greatest names in photography are represented here: Nadar, Muybridge and Roger Fenton from the early days of the medium; Alfred Stieglitz, Edward Weston, Imogen Cunningham, Man Ray, Hoyningen-Huene, Frantisek Drtikol, Germaine Krull; from our own time, John Coplans, Robert Mapplethorpe, Richard Hamilton, Sally Mann, Helen Chadwick, Barbara Kruger, Cindy Sherman, Pierre Radisic, Dieter Appelt and many others. Also included are works by artists who have used the body itself as their medium and means of expression, such as Carolee Schneemann, Bruce Nauman, Arnulf Rainer and Robert Morris.

WOMEN ARTISTS AND WRITERS Modernist (im)positionings by Bridget Elliott and Jo-Ann Wallace, Routledge, 204pp, b/w ills, HB £40/PB £15.99

Bridget Elliot and Jo-Ann Wallace reappraise the literary and artistic contribution of women to modernism and in particular the self representation and construction of artistic identity. They put forward a powerful case against the academic 'disciplining' of cultural production into departments of Art History and English Studies which has served to marginalise the work of female modernists. Taking a comparative case study approach the authors examine the ways in which women, including Natalie Barney, Virginia Woolf, Vanessa Bell and Gertrude Stein, responded to modernism and the manner in which their work has been positioned in relation to that of men. These comparisions reveal different methods of achieving similar aims: Marie Laurencin produced representations of women that were hyperbolically 'feminine' and not obviously progressive, while Gertrude Stein identified with masculine models of artistic genius and yet left an 'important and enabling' body of lesbian love poetry. In the past, academic analyses of feminism have been treated in a disinterested or superficial manner. This book engages with the subject and allows for the idiosyncratic in a way which brings these women alive.

PLASTICS Plastics from the Greek word Plastikos – Mouldable by Lena Rahoult, Carouschka, Ruch Ltd, Cultural Centre, Stockholm, Beate Sydhoff, Sissi Nilsson, Design Museum, London, 128pp, colour ills, HB £19.99

This book studies the archaeology of plastics – from the first mass-produced objects made of Bakelite to the sophisticated variety of plastic products in use in medicine and communication today. Natural polymers such as lacquer, amber and horn were first used, but in 1530, the German alchemist Bartholomäus Schobinger invented a recipe for making casein plastic from cheese to replace horn for marquetry work. Like other forms of archaeology, plastic archaeology is distinguished by those who discovered each product lending

it their name. In 1823 Charles Macintosh made the first raincoat from natural rubber and in 1839 ironmonger Charles Goodyear inadvertently invented vulcanisation. Plastics within the field of medicine have achieved considerable success: in the 1940s a British ophthalmologist realised that fragments of windshield in a pilot's eye caused only a slight reaction and the same plastic was used to replace lenses. Plastic is the ultimate consumer material and its disposable nature fits the high demands on hygiene made in the health care area but research is being carried out into sustainable biodegradability.

LOOKING AT GIACOMETTI by David Sylvester, Chatto and Windus, 250pp, b/w ills, HB £25

This unusually profound response to Alberto Giacometti's art is the fruit of a prolonged collaboration with Giacometti as sitter, friend, critic and exhibition curator. Unlike many less thorough critics, David Sylvester describes Giacometti's etiolated figures as 'figures without "physical superfluousness" like Starbuck in *Moby Dick*, their thinness a condensation'. Written over a period of 40 years from Sylvester's first visits to Giacometti's studio in the late forties, to his prolonged sitting for Giacometti's portrait of him in 1960, up to his meditations on the artist's completed oeuvre after his death. The book is comprised of a mixture of biography and criticism and it includes an interview with Giacometti. The biography reveals that after his surrealist sculptures of the 1930s, he suddenly isolated himself and began obsessively to make and re-make sculptures and paintings wrestling with complex problems of perception and representation. By the mid-1950s he had established his reputation as one of most startlingly original and important artists of the 20th century.

EGYPTOMANIA The Egyptian Revival: a Recurring Theme in the History of Taste by James Stevens Curl, 298pp, b/w ills, HB £50/PB £16.99

James Stevens Curl suggests that the Egyptian Revival manifested itself in the 20th century in the Art Deco Style. The discovery of the

tomb of Tutankhamun in 1922 was an archaeological triumph which had an enormous effect on the arts of Europe and America. Modern publicity enabled customisation of this 'Nile Style' and a rejuvenated form of 18th century Egyptomania infused all levels of culture and Egyptianising motifs. This appeared in objects 'from ash-trays to cinemas, from jewellery to furniture, from suburban drawing rooms to company boardrooms'. Stevens Curl argues that these motifs were essential ingredients of the democratising of art through the 1925 Exposition International des Arts Decoratifs et Industriels Modernes. This, the dawn of Art Deco was combined with the discovery of new modern materials which meant that Egyptian artefacts could be copied in new materials such as Bakelite.

THE ROMANTIC SPIRIT IN GERMAN ART 1790-1990 edited by Keith Hartley, Henry Meyric Hughes, Peter-Klaus Shuster and William Vaughan, Hayward Gallery, South Bank Centre, London and Scottish National Gallery of Modern Art, Edinburgh, 500pp, colour ills, PB £26.50

Like the exhibition this book studies the influence of Romanticism on the development of German art over the past 200 years and explores its relationship with modernism. Over 40 essays discuss movements in German art chronologically from Romanticism, Symbolism, Modernism (Expressionism, Dada, Bauhaus, Neue Schlichkeit) to Art in the Third Reich and Post-War art. The principal themes of the Romantic movement – the individual's relationship to society, nature and the cosmos and the superiority of instinct and feeling over reason and 'civilisation' – are illustrated in the works of Philipp Otto Runge, Friedrich Schinkel , Caspar David Friedrich and the Nazarenes. It focuses on the Symbolists and the exponents of the Modern Movement: Emile Nolde, Franz Marc, Wassily Kandinsky, Paul Klee and finally those exponents of the art of the Third Reich: Oskar Martin-Amorbach and Adolf Wissel and onwards to Joseph Beuys, Anselm Kiefer, Sigmar Polke.

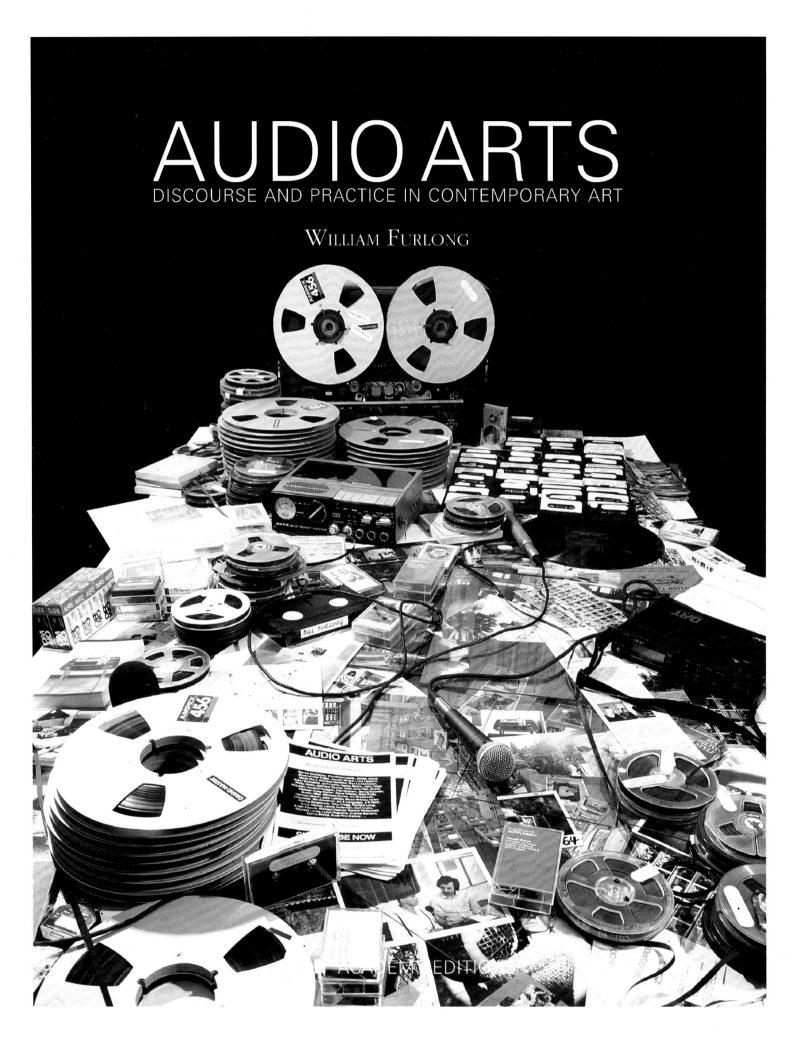

AUDIO ARTS

DISCOURSE AND PRACTICE IN CONTEMPORARY ART

William Furlong

AUDIO ARTS

LAUNCH AT THE SERPENTINE GALLERY, LONDON

The launch of a new book on the internationally renowned Audio Arts was celebrated with the kind permission of the Serpentine Gallery, London, on September 13th, 1994. It was an important moment for William Furlong, who began the project in 1973 with Barry Barker. Audio Arts was conceived as a work of art in itself. It was the first art magazine to be published on audio cassette. It is now an invaluable source of reference about contemporary art of the last 20 years. Furlong was joined by, among others: Michael Archer, Furlong's principal collaborator throughout the 1980s; John Walters, the former BBC radio producer who broadcast Audio Arts in the 1980s on his programme 'Walters Weekly'; Mel Gooding, who wrote the introductory essay 'The Work' – which establishes the creative-critical position of Audio Arts in the mid 90s; Lewis Johnston, former director of the Lewis Johnston Gallery which was active in early 1980s London, and Marjorie Allthorpe-Guyton, Art Director of the Arts Council of Great Britain and former editor of *Artscribe International*. Bruce McLean, Michael Archer, Mel Gooding and John Walters made speeches about the book to mark the event, excerpts from which appear here.

Paperback 1-85490-363-2
279x217 mm, 144 pages
100 illustrations in colour and black and white

Bruce McLean

I think what is so great about Audio Arts is its sheer insanity: only a mad man could have contemplated such relentless attention to what is happening. The best thing about Bill Furlong is that in spite of all that work, he has always been on hand and willing to collaborate with me on performances and recordings: to help me and other artists make their own work. Yes, it is a work, a terrific project – keep going . . .

Michael Archer

From the outset I was interested in Audio Arts for the different kind of space it seemed to provide. Its use of recording technology established an environment into which both artworks and ideas about them could be introduced. Thus, although Bill was an artist, and I wanted to produce criticism, it was clear that both approaches could be accommodated within the ambience of the Audio Arts project. It remains equally clear that that project was, and is, Bill's. One of its many strengths is that throughout the years of my collaboration I have not felt my contribution to be merely a subordinate one. The space Audio Arts offers is an enabling one.

Mel Gooding

Audio Arts is more than a cassette magazine – it has become a great work of the creative imagination: Unprecedented in its scale and range, it reflects the response of a truly original artist, over 20 years of work, and the visual art of our time . . . I am convinced, Audio Arts is a major work of art.

John Walters

When I had a programme on BBC Radio 1 I started to come across artists' work in sound and put out some, but then discovered that Bill Furlong of Audio Arts was there already, doing it . . . so I worked with him on numerous occasions from then on.

A Picasso Bestiary
Neil Cox and Deborah Povey

Picasso was fascinated by animals and many of his most intriguing and stimulating creations represent beasts in all manner of guises, both serious and playful. *A Picasso Bestiary* published to coincide with the exhibition 'Cock and Bull Stories: A Picasso Bestiary held at Croydon in 1995, gathers together a selection of Picasso's animal works grouped by subject: The Bull, The Horse, Birds, Cats and Dogs, Sheep and Goats, Watery Creatures, Insects, Monkeys and Monsters. This format was suggested by the structure of the mediaeval bestiary: a luxurious 'Book of Beasts' which described the wonders of the animal kingdom and explained their moral and spiritual significance.

This book is uniquely comprised of two narratives, one dealing with a tradition of animal representation and the other with Picasso. Their juxtaposition, together with a wealth of visual material, allows exciting patterns to emerge which demonstrate both how consistently certain long-established themes continue into Picasso's art, and how wilfully others are abandoned in favour of his own personal vision.

A Picasso Bestiary
Neil Cox and Deborah Povey
PICASSO

Paperback 1 85490 401 9
279 x 217mm, 208 pages
250 illustrations, 100 colour
March 1995

Journal of Philosophy & The Visual Arts No. 5
Abstraction

Edited by Andrew Benjamin

Abstraction has not only been an important 20th-century art form but has also given rise to one of the most significant and influential schools of criticism. It has almost become inseparable from its critical reception. Rather than accepting this as given, and thus as inevitable, this issue of the *Journal of Philosophy & The Visual Arts* will seek to offer different interpretations of abstraction. Texts by some of the leading philosophers and critics writing today, including Jean-François Lyotard, Thierry de Duve, Stan Allen, John Rajchman, Andrew Benjamin, Maia Damianovic and John Lechte, accompany features on work by some of the leading artists working currently in the field of abstraction, including Gerhard Richter, Lydia Dona, David Reed, Jonathan Lasker, Fiona Rae, Therese Oulton and Jessica Stockholder.

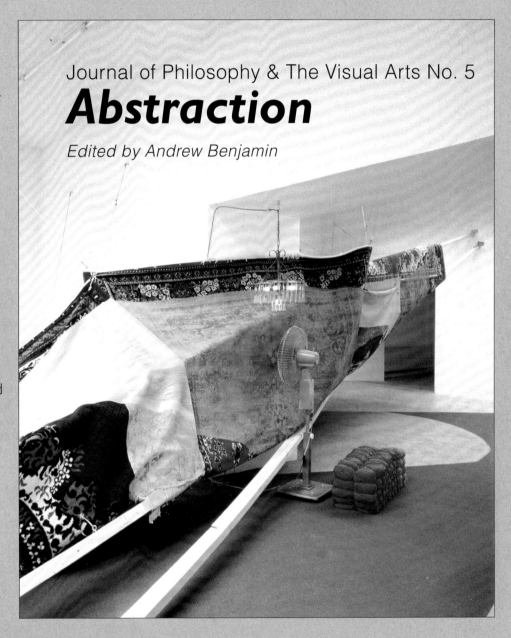

Journal of Philosophy & The Visual Arts No. 5
Abstraction

Edited by Andrew Benjamin

Paperback   1 85490 402 7
279x217mm, 96 pages
30 ills colour and b&w
April 1995

'Jérôme and Sylvie

did not quite believe that

you could go into battle

for a chesterfield settee.

But that was the

the banner under which

they would have enlisted

most readily'.

Georges Perec, *Things*, 1965

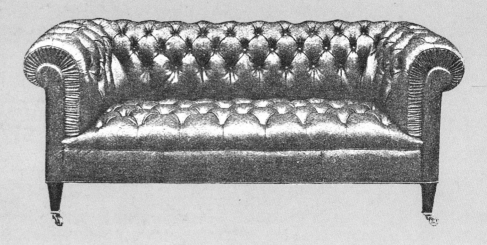

THE CONTEMPORARY SUBLIME
SENSIBILITIES OF TRANSCENDENCE AND SHOCK

Abigail Lane, The Incident Room (detail), *1993*

Art & Design

THE CONTEMPORARY SUBLIME
SENSIBILITIES OF TRANSCENDENCE AND SHOCK

Terry Shave, Estuary Series, *1990; OPPOSITE: Ashley Bickerton*, Solomon Island Shark, *1993*

ACADEMY EDITIONS • LONDON

Acknowledgements

We would like to thank Dr Paul Crowther for guest-editing this special issue of *Art & Design* on the Sublime. Unless otherwise stated, all images are courtesy of the artists. *p1* courtesy of Glenn Scott Wright, London; *p2* 'Some Went Mad . . . Some Ran Away . . .' Serpentine Gallery, London, 1994; **Introduction** *pp6-7: p6* Marlborough Fine Art, London, photo Prudence Cuming; **The Sublime is How** *pp18-33: p24* photo Otto Neoleon; **Kant and Malevich** *pp34-41: pp35, 37, 39* State Russia Museum, Leningrad; **Damien Hirst and the Sensibilities of Shock** *pp54-67: pp54, 57, 62, 64* White Cube Gallery, London, *pp54, 57* photos Jay Jopling, *p62* photo André Morin Le Jeune, *pp56, 60, 65* Saatchi Collection, London, *p65* photo Glenn Scott Wright, London; *p66* Serpentine Gallery, London; **Silent Visions** *pp68-75: pp68, 70* Albright Knox Art Gallery, Buffalo, *p70* collection of Mr and Mrs Paul Mellon, National Gallery of Art, Washington DC; *p74* Museum of Modern Art, New York

COVER: Cornelia Parker, Matter and What it Means, *1989, photo Edward Woodman*
INSIDE COVERS: Yves Klein, La Lune I, *1961, Kunstsammlung NRW, Düsseldorf*
PAGE 5: Barnett Newman, Canto VII, *1963, Tate Gallery, London*

HOUSE EDITOR: Nicola Hodges EDITORIAL TEAM: Iona Spens, Ramona Khambatta
ART EDITOR: Andrea Bettella CHIEF DESIGNER: Mario Bettella DESIGNER: Jan Richter

First published in Great Britain in 1995 by *Art & Design* an imprint of
ACADEMY GROUP LTD, 42 LEINSTER GARDENS, LONDON W2 3AN
Member of the VCH Publishing Group
ISBN: 1 85490 223 7 (UK)

Art & Design Profile 40 is published as part of *Art & Design* Vol 10 1/2 1995
Art & Design Magazine is published six times a year and is available by subscription

Distributed to the trade in the United States of America by
ST MARTIN'S PRESS, 175 FIFTH AVENUE, NEW YORK, NY 10010

Printed and bound in Italy

Contents

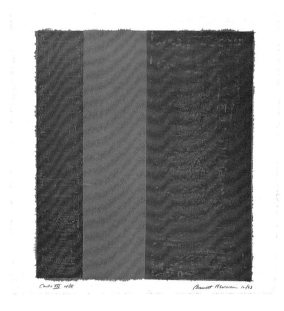

ART & DESIGN PROFILE No 40

Guest Edited by Paul Crowther

THE CONTEMPORARY SUBLIME
SENSIBILITIES OF TRANSCENDENCE AND SHOCK

INTRODUCTION

Paul Crowther

In the past decade there has been considerable talk about the importance of the 'spiritual' in art (as opposed, say to the concepts of theories in terms of which it is to be negotiated). However, it is much harder to pin down what is actually meant by the term 'spiritual' itself, in the artistic context. Often it seems to mean little more than the fact that art still remains (somehow) connected to self-expression.

However, there is at least one aspect of the 'spiritual' which can be made specific. In his book *Modern Painting and the Northern Romantic Tradition*, Robert Rosenblum traces a continuing tradition in art from the 18th century to the 1960s, which centres upon the term 'sublime'. Sublimity in this familiar artistic sense involves characteristically large canvases which, through evocations of wild natural grandeur, limitlessness, or intense painterly means, seek to express ultimate truths about the individual's relation to the world.

Now in the 1980s and 90s something of this tradition has continued, albeit (in some cases) in an extremely modified form. Perhaps the closest point of contact between the old and the new in this respect, is the work of Thérese Oulton, which draws some of its resources from the likes of Constable and Turner, as well as the American colour-field painters of the 1950s and 60s. Another familiar example of this sort is the work of Anselm Kiefer. His vast canvases alluding to the disasters of German history and national identity are very much what we would expect of 'sublime' painting,

as are some of his more recent works focusing on mythological or cosmological imagery.

Both Oulton and Kiefer, of course, not only build on this tradition, they also change it – sometimes in startling ways. Similar considerations hold in relation to recent works by Gerhard Richter, Georg Baselitz, Walter de Maria, James Turrell and Ian Hamilton Finlay.

The present edition of *Art & Design* will, of course, address aspects of this mainstream of tradition, and its new creative tributaries. However, the intellectual task it sets itself is rather broader. It will seek specifically to situate works within the context of *theories* of the sublime, notably those proposed by Burke and Kant. In this respect, it is worth noting even now, that Burke's theory is organised around the positive significance of shock and horror, whereas Kant's involves a rational containment of excess which leads to a kind of transcending of the mundane self. This latter theory is especially fruitful since it points us towards realms of experience which border on, or overlap with, the sublime – religious awareness is one of these, and the organisation of memory through artistic means is another. Kant's theory is also of great use in establishing connections between the sublime and the art formats and strategies which have come to the fore during the last decade.

It is hoped, then, that by considering the sublime in a contemporary context, familiar material will be illuminated, and new possibilities encompassed.

Thérese Oulton, Saturations No 4, 1992, oil on canvas.

THE POSTMODERN SUBLIME
INSTALLATION AND ASSEMBLAGE ART
Paul Crowther

Whether or not they have now exceeded their high point of influence, deconstructive strategies of one sort or another have dominated recent innovatory thought in the humanities and social sciences. At the heart of all these strategies is one major insight – that the meaningfulness of an item is not determined by direct unmediated correspondence between (in the very broadest terms) concept and object. Rather the relation between these elements is unstable, and determined by its position within an overall field of signification. This field itself, however, is not an enclosed totality. It is open and subject to constant reconfiguration.

Now there are, of course, many different inflections of this general position. In Lacan's work, for example, it is expressed in the way that language's differential structure is seen as embodying – and, indeed, perpetuating – a lack of congruence between thought or desire and its objects. In Derrida's writing it is argued that Western thought is dominated by a 'logocentric' prejudice, wherein the field of linguistic meaning is unwarrantably assimilated to the supposedly direct relation which holds between the individual speech-act and the 'presence' of its semantic content. Again, in Foucault the notion of 'discourse' is fundamental. A 'discourse' is not a once-and-for-all given body of universal truths. Rather it is a specific (historically transformable) field wherein meaning is produced solely in a context determined by relations of power organised on the basis of class, gender, race, religion and the like.

There is one key point to grasp from this brief survey. If (as in all the above views) meaning is only producible within an unstable field, then the relation of self to work, and self to its own self-understanding, are both, at best, provisional. Their 'essence' is to be constantly re-made, as the overall field of meaning itself undergoes reconfiguration. The self and its position in the world have no fixed centre; they are 'ex-centric'.

The question now arises as to whether this deconstructive impulse is just another intellectual fad, or something of much broader significance. A partial answer to this is found in Jean-Francois Lyotard's exhibition *Les Immateriaux*, held at the Centre Georges Pompidou in 1985. At the heart of this exhibition was a thesis concerning technology and humanity. It is well summarised in Walter Benjamin's observation that, in the era of mass-reproduction of images, 'technology has subjected the human sensorium to a complex kind of training'.[1] Lyotard's exhibition went a good way towards clarifying some of the many aspects of this training. Specifically, it evoked the way in which the availability of information, and the complex new modes of obtaining and transmitting it, transform both human understanding and the object of such understanding. The exhibition consisted of 31 zones (some subdivided) yielding a total of over 60 sites. The viewer was free to wander through this labyrinth according to his or her own order of priorities, accompanied only by a set of headphones. On entering each zone, the headphones would pick up a 'commentary' for that zone, consisting of music, or readings from poetry, philosophy or other kinds of text.

The overall organisational principle of the exhibition centred on the notion of the 'message'. This involved the interplay of five factors – the origin of the message, its medium, the code of articulation, the 'content' of the message, and, of course, its ultimate destination. These factors were explored in relation to computer and media technology, art, ideas of gender, and many other aspects of postmodern life. The upshot was a sense that, in present times, the everyday surface of life is dematerialised. That which once was simply present to consciousness, is, in the context of information deriving from new technologies, now seen to be a function of more complex relations. The material world is, as it were, a projection from this domain of 'immaterials'. Its meaning is no longer perceived; rather it has to be *deciphered* in relation to the broader network of relation which subtend it.

There are a number of points to gather from all this. First, it is clear that the deconstructive impulse outlined earlier is more than a fad. It is part of a much broader transformation intimately connected with social and technological change. This connection should not be construed in a causal sense, ie the deconstructive impulse is not just a 'reflection' of deeper transformations of socio-economic factors. The situation is *much* more

Cornelia Parker, Cold Dark Matter – An Exploded View, *1991. OPPOSITE: Detail of contents of the garden shed, focusing on the bulb; ABOVE: View of the shed in Chisenhale Gallery, prior to the explosion*

complicated. Something of this complexity can be understood through the theory of Jean Baudrillard. He argues that the boundaries between consciousness, its products, and reality, have been totally erased. There is no more nature, no more reality as such. How we represent the world, and, in particular, how we represent it through media-messages, has totally colonised any sense of what the world is, in itself. We are now in the realm of the 'hyperreal'. Baudrillard indicates some of the factors involved here as follows: 'all hold-ups, hi-jacks and the like are now as it were simulation hold-ups, in the sense that they are inscribed in advance in the decoding and orchestration rituals of the media, anticipated in their mode of presentation and possible consequences. In brief [they] function as a set of signs dedicated exclusively to their recurrence as signs, no longer to their "real" goal at all'.[2]

These points can be further illuminated by a recent example. In early 1994 the far-right Afrikaner group, the AWB, organised a terror-convoy of cars, which drove through a black township in South Africa, firing indiscriminately. (This, in itself, or course, is an excellent example of the action-as-media-spectacle just described by Baudrillard.) The tail end of the convoy, however, was hit by return gunfire from black policemen. Two wounded Afrikaners – despite their pleas for mercy – were then shot dead by one of the policemen, quite cold-bloodedly, in front of TV cameras and photographers. In effect, this was a murder done *for the purpose of media-transmission*. Now when the reporting of this event was considered by a panel of 'critics' on the BBC's *Late Show*, the shocking aspect of the event was accounted for purely on the basis of the racial insecurity of whites encountering a show of newly attained black power. Rather than address the question of murder for media-entertainment, in other words, the critics assimilated the event in terms of the fashionable chatter codes of political correctness.

All these considerations must now be placed in a much broader perspective. Lyotard's *Les Immateriaux*, and Baudrillard's hyper-reality show how the deconstructive tendencies look in relation to a broader play of constantly changing codes and signifying practices. What kind of sensibility does this engender? One aspect of it is clearly an ever-accelerating demand for the new and unexpected. Sensationalism (especially as provided by the media) does not simply play its traditional modern role of offering a break from the routine continuum of life; rather it is an *addiction*. This even extends to the domain of art. For whilst novelties, outrage and scandal have always been an important element in Modernism, in

postmodernism they are demanded almost as a matter of course. And this, of course, drives art and its critics to greater extremes. We need the likes of Damien Hirst and Robert Mapplethorpe to satisfy our cravings.

There is another aspect to contemporary sensibility. The diversity and excess of information and possible standpoints (especially in relation to questions of taste) has become something which can be enjoyed in its own right. In this respect, the rise of the installation and site-specific assemblages as distinctive artistic formats, is significant in itself. There are, of course, precedents for these, notably in Dada and Surrealist 'manifestations'. However it is only since the 1960s that temporary installations or assemblages have become commonplace artistic practice. To some degree this might be explained in terms of a greater interest in theoretical issues amongst artists and critics. However, it can also be seen as another manifestation of the deconstructive tendencies noted earlier. For the very essence of these formats is to create a meaningful configuration whose meaning is inescapably determined by a field of relations. The conventional art object is also determined in these terms; but in the installation and assemblage it is made much more overt. The work comes to us in a context where the transience of the specific configuration is known in advance. We know that the work will cease to be, and that something else will come to occupy its space. Installation and assemblage, in other words, are formats where the art object is overtly 'ex-centric'.

Both aspects of contemporary sensibility which have just outlined have been related elsewhere (by myself and many others[3]) to the experience of the sublime. There are two *basic* varieties of such experience, whose credentials have been broadly presented by Burke and Kant respectively. Burke's sublime is fundamentally an existential one. For him, we enjoy the sensory overload of vast objects, or the threat of dangerous ones (when encountered from a position of safely) precisely because the shock they give us revivifies our sense of being alive. In such contexts, Burke informs us that, 'if the pain or terror are so modified as not to be actually noxious; if the pain is not carried to violence, and the terror is not conversant about the present destruction of the person, as these emotions clear the parts of a troublesome encumbrance, they are capable of producing delight; not pleasure, but a sort of delightful horror . . .'[4]

This mode of sublimity relates most directly to the sensationalist aspect of contemporary sensibility noted earlier. It raises, however, the question of moral insensitivity. For an experience of this sort

Cornelia Parker, Cold Dark Matter – An Exploded View, *1991, the garden shed awaiting explosion*

can be stimulated by images of warfare and destruction and the like, making us inert to the real moral issues involved in this kind of spectatorship. (*The Late Show* critics – also noted earlier – are clear victims of this inertness.) However, this does not have to be the case. Leon Golub's paintings of torture victims and torturers, for example, involve the protagonists staring directly at the viewer. The torturers smirk, and present themselves *as* performers for the media-gaze. In this way, the shock value of the work is brought to a point of critical reflection. One is invited to question the degree to which one's fascination with the horrible spectacle is complicit with the deed enacted. For example, it may be that the torturer plays and enjoys his 'role', by conforming to the sadistic torturer image which is a mainstay of so many violent action films.

The other dimension of the sublime which is often linked to contemporary culture, is much more complex. It is articulated in Kant's critical philosophy, and part of its complexity is a function of the difficulty of Kant's own exposition of it.[5] His starting point is a definition of the sublime as that which is 'absolutely' and 'beyond all comparison' great. There is only one thing which can satisfy this definition – our rational (and, in Kant's terms, moral) capacities. These are the 'supersensible' aspects of the self, ie that source of decision-making and thinking whose workings cannot be reduced to the causal mechanisms of nature. The reason why this alone warrants the term 'sublime' is precisely that it is beyond nature and the sensible world. For any individual item which occurs in that world – no matter how vast or mighty it may be – there is always some other item in relation to which its vastness and power is small. Only that which is beyond the *measurable* world of nature, can claim to be great beyond comparison. Our rational capacities have this status. For they are not only outside nature, but can, through thought, comprehend the idea of infinity itself.

Now for Kant, an awareness of the scope of these capacities can be arrived at from two different directions. In the 'mathematical sublime' a *vast* object overwhelms our perceptual and imaginative capacities. We simply cannot comprehend it as a totality at the level of the senses. However, no matter how vast the thing may be, we can comprehend it at the level of thought. Indeed, our very inability to wholly assimilate it at the sensory level, makes the fact that we can thus assimilate it in rational terms all the more vivid. We come to *feel* the scope and superiority of our rational being.

The other route to this awareness arises from our encounter with enormously *powerful* things. It is the 'dynamical sublime'. Kant's treatment of this is

rather contorted, and is needlessly at odds with his account of the mathematical mode. However, it can be more consistently stated as follows. An item of immense power is one whose full workings and potentially destructive effects are such that we could never take them in (in any complete way) in terms of perception and imagination. We can, nevertheless, comprehend such might at the level of ideas – in rational terms – and, again, the sensory incomprehensibility of the object serves to vivify the scope of such rational comprehension.

In Kant's account, these experiences of the sublime arise exclusively from our engagement with nature. Art – as a product of human artifice – is readily comprehensible in both perceptual/imaginative *and* rational terms, and so lacks that zone of conflict wherein lack at the former level serves to make us feel the superiority of the latter. However, Kant is, I think, again not completely consistent on this, and it is possible to argue a case (as I have done at length elsewhere[6]) for viably linking art and sublimity in a number of ways.

There is one major point to gather from all these considerations. In Kant's terms the sublime hinges on a relation between perceptual and imaginative *excess* and rational *containment*. It is the generality of this relation which gives the Kantian sublime such a broad potential application. We will recall that earlier on I linked contemporary culture to deconstructive tendencies and Baudrillard's 'hyperreal'. On these terms, the boundaries between self and world are dissolved in the 'play' of signs and representations. We have an *excess* of images and signs. But why is it that we are not simply lost in all this? Why, indeed, is it possible to enjoy the whole spectacle? I would answer: because it is sublime in the Kantian sense. The sensory and imaginative excess can be comprehended as an idea. It revivifies our capacity for rational insight – our very ability to create and discover meaning. In a curious way, indeed, this aesthetic response to the patterns of contemporary culture, is one which can resist their potentially desensitising and dehumanising effects. Installation and assemblage art can be especially potent in this respect. I shall now consider a few possibilities.

First, Lyotard's *Les Immateriaux* exhibition presented contemporary culture as a spectacle; and whilst criticisms could be made of it, it invited a questioning of that culture through the overt excessivenes of the whole spectacle. Indeed, even as one was overwhelmed by the labyrinth of images and information, one knew that it had been brought forth – like all the products of culture – by human powers of rational ingenuity.

This possibility for critical reflection within the

Cornelia Parker, Cold Dark Matter – An Exploded View, *1991. ABOVE: The shed being blown up by army explosives; OVERLEAF: The restructured shed in the Chisenhale Gallery*

aesthetic can also be discerned on a much less extravagant scale in the work of particular artists. For example, David Mach's work throughout the 1980s and 90s has centred on site-specific assemblages where an overriding image is composed from ready-made units. (He has used, for example, tyres, toys, magazines, bottles, kitchen and household utensils, footwear and so on.) Now whereas, say, an artist such as Jeff Koons exploits such banal items for weak theoretical ends, Mach does not. Rather, the emphasis in his work is on the fragile relation between the constituent units and the image which, in concert, they represent. There is, of course, a great deal of irony and humour in many of these conjunctions, but this aspect is of broader significance. For it is achieved through the *manipulation* of an excess of ready-made signs. It contains and controls these signs. Humour and irony in this context, in other words, are a vivid exemplar of the triumph of reason over the excess of banality. We have a kind of critical/comical version of the sublime.

The Slovenian duo VSSD have produced some of the most impressive installation art of the 1990s. One might consider, for example, *(About) The Soul* – an installation at the Equirna Gallery, Ljubljana, in early 1994. For this work, selected areas of the gallery walls were painted blue and hung with numerous small paintings of flames and fractal patterns. In the centre of the main space, a small group of glasses was assembled; each glass was partially broken and painted in black. In an antechamber to the main space a series of tables and chairs were placed, together with copies of precious VSSD writings and catalogues. The title of the work alludes to Aristotle's *De Anima (On the Soul)*; and the nature of the self and identity form the real substance of this installation. The term 'substance' is especially pertinent in this context. Traditional notions of the self or soul construe it as a simple individual substance. However, as we have already seen, the self in contemporary times is seen in much more complex 'ex-centric' terms; and this is exactly how it is treated in *(About) The Soul*. The self is de-substantialised through resolution into an ill-defined field of constituent elements, whose individual significance is also ambiguous. The small paintings, for example, are like particular memories. They are different from one another in literal terms; but they have strong *stylistic* affinities. Indeed, since the self is not just the sum of its memory-parts, how we read these parts individually and in concert, is determined by their relation to a *whole* which encompasses, of course, factors beyond the individual self. The ambiguity of this wholeness – this enmeshing of inside and outside –

was brought out by the overall physical layout of the installation, encompassing, as it did, different formats in different rooms with no linear narrative to connect our traversals of them.

Interestingly, as well as thematising the complexity of the self *per se*, *(About) The Soul* also declares the problems of VSSD's own identity. The particular configuration of the whole installation was new, but it did not simply come to be *ex-nihilo*. This was shown, in part, by the presence of the VSSD catalogues as an integral element in the installation; but more significantly it was a function of the small memory-analogue paintings just mentioned. The flames and fractals were disposed in a new way, but they are important and familiar VSSD motifs from previous installations. They therefore exemplified the continuity and difference which characterises both individual and group identity.

Now in one sense, a work such as *(About) The Soul* overwhelms with its many-layered complexity. At the same time, however, it is both a containment and elucidation of that complexity. Again, it makes vivid the scope of reason itself.

All the factors which I have been considering in relation to installation and assemblage art meet in the work of one of the most outstanding recent practitioners of these idioms – Cornelia Parker. The bulk of her most impressive installation involved items suspended – quite visible and palpably – by wires from the ceilings of gallery spaces. The objects she uses are ready-made – coins, household appliances, toys, trophies, silver-plate etc – very much the kind of bric-a-brac one might encounter in junk shops and car-boot sales. This detritus of consumer society, however, is subjected by her to decisive transformation. Consider the following remarks: 'I'm concerned with ambivalence, with opposites, with inhaling and exhaling, things falling apart and things rising, things disintegrating and coming back together . . . with killing things off, as it they existed in cartoon comics and then resurrecting them, so that one set of references is negated as a new one takes its place'.[7]

These strategies can be well illustrated by a few examples. In an installation created in 1989 (entitled *Matter and What it Means*) Parker had five thousand coins flattened into slivers by a steamroller. The slivers were then suspended by wire (a short distance above the ground) so as to give the impression of two human forms, hovering in space. Here a number of avenues of association converge. All matter can be resolved into simpler elements; these are gathered together when a form comes into being, and fall apart when the form ceases to be. A simple fact. But Parker's installation locates the spectator in a space between the

FROM ABOVE: VSSD, It is Accomplished, The Future is Superfluous, *space painting in the middle of space; VSSD,* (About) The Soul, *1994, Equirna Gallery, Ljubljana*

two factors of cohesion and resolution. It is a space of relationships which define life and death itself. Another aspect of this is illuminated in the relation of the suspended figures and the shadows they cast upon the ground. We see the figure as inhabiting both an overt present and an obscure or hidden past simultaneously. Indeed, the way the figures hover over the ground conveys a sense of the individual, the species, and (again) of life itself as having emerged from an anonymous matrix.

The more cosmological implications of these themes are well brought out in what is arguably Parker's most spectacular installation to date – *Cold Dark Matter – An Exploded View*, 1991. This work was commissioned by the Chisenhale Gallery, which has placed itself at the forefront of experimental presentations. The first gallery-based stage of the installation consisted of a garden shed (lit from the inside), occupying an otherwise empty floorspace. In this context, the object was endowed with an eerie sense of something 'about to happen'. And it did. Parker had the shed and its contents (diverse bric-a-brac of the kind noted earlier) transported to an outdoor location. It was then blown up by army explosives experts, with the explosion captured on film. Parker collected the debris, and, suspended from wires, it came to form the final stage of the gallery installation. The hanging of the damaged material and debris was guided by photographs of the explosion itself, with a 200-watt light bulb at the heart of the suspended assemblage. The result was both a constellation of material and an extraordinary play of shadows about the gallery walls and floorspace.

The cosmological symbolism of *Cold Dark Matter* . . . again involves a convergence of kindred associations. There is an obvious allusion to the Big Bang, and, in the fact that the suspended material has undergone a form of destruction (and is now useless), to an ultimate contraction and disintegration. What is of more interest is the universal constant which this specific cosmological pairing involves. Parker professes an interest in opposites and the like, and links *Cold Dark Matter* . . . to inhaling and exhaling. But again this opposition is a particular manifestation of a more universal relation of convergence and divergence, centripetal and centrifugal motion. This rhythm of opposition is at the heart of all Being. Indeed its recurrent character is suggested by the play of shadows from the assemblage. The forces which sustain its configuration have operated before, and will operate again. The shadows are hence the latent space of past actualities and future possibilities.

One further universal factor in Parker's work must now be considered. The relation between contingency and necessity is one of the most fundamental of all the oppositions which inform human experience. *Cold Dark Matter* . . . explores this in interesting ways. At first sight it is mere chaos. Then we see the strings and recognise the imposition of order. Now all art (except the most vacuous experiments with pure chance) involves giving some form to material, but the process of making or arranging involves contingent elements of choice. (In the present case, even if Parker had arranged the debris so as to exactly reconfigure a specific moment in the explosive dispersal, there would still be some ambiguity – some contingent element of choice involved.) However, in the final product all is necessity. The many different possible routes to the made object or installation end here. From the viewpoint of the end product, the contingencies of the process of creation now appear inexorable. This fact is true of all art, but in the work of an artist such as Parker, it is elevated from the realm of the unrecognised or intuitive, to become a *thematic* element in the work itself. What is especially subtle is the particular means whereby Parker achieved this. For the contingent material she is dealing with is manifestly – through the marks of damage and destruction – shaped by the blind causal forces of natural necessity. And whilst the final assemblage is necessary (in the sense noted earlier) it has the appearance of being a merely chaotic configuration. Here in other words, contingency and necessity do not occur in some neat well-defined opposition, rather, as in lived experience itself, they weave imperceptibly in and out of one another.

The final comment which I shall make in relation to Parker's work concerns its origins. She is fascinated by children's encyclopaedias, and especially those images and diagrams which 'unpack' an object or phenomenon, showing us all the many different elements which it contains. Similarly she is fascinated by those processes of change and destruction in cartoons, whereby say, Tom is battered out of shape by Jerry, only to reassume his original form a few moments later. Now Parker's creative impulse is one which radiates outwards from these simulacra or caricatures of objects and events. She takes simple (sometimes banal) structures and 'resurrects' them in a way which brings out much deeper levels of significance. To engage with her work in aesthetic terms is, at the same time, to be brought to a point of critical reflection.

It is now time to gather the overall salient points of this discussion together. First, I outlined the prevalence of deconstructionist tendencies in contemporary thought, and suggested that these can be linked to much broader patterns of societal and

VSSD, (About) The Soul, 1994, Equirna Gallery, Ljubljana

technological change. It was also argued that these patterns sustain a distinctive contemporary sensibility oriented on the one hand towards shock and sensation and, on the other towards an aesthetic of contained excess. This latter aspect involves a kind of pleasure in deconstruction, which can be broadly understood on the model of Kant's theory of the sublime. Installation and assemblage has a special role in this respect in so far as it hinges on the relation between containment and excess – the basis of the Kantian sublime. However it is important to end with points of both qualification and elucidation.

The qualification consists in this. There is a clear link to be made between the Kantian sublime and contemporary art. But it should not be thought that an installation or assemblage or, indeed, any aesthetic response to a contemporary phenomenon must therefore be characterised as 'sublime'. For this term to be used, we really *must* be engaging with works which, through testing our perceptual or imaginative resources, at the same time makes the scope of rational comprehension more vivid. This is not just a case of something being big or complicated. It requires something else determined by our cultural context. It requires mediation by a sense of what is important, problematic, or even dangerous in our broader contemporary scheme of interests. We need to be positioned. This is why I have considered artists whose work invites critical reflection. Their particular modes of installing or assembling are ones where the kind of

excess and complexity contained, and more significantly, the particular strategy of rational containment involved, are ones which matter to us *now*. Living in a culture where 'loss of self' is a constant threat, the critical reflections of Mach, VSSD and Parker each give us (in different ways) a position from which the self's relation to the world can be understood and thence stabilised.

We are thus led to the point of elucidation. The deconstructive and hyper-real tendencies with their 'ex-centricity' of self and world are amongst the pre-conditions for the sensibility and art which I have described. However, the art (at least) does not simply reflect those conditions; it even – to some degree – subverts them. For whilst the self may be, in important senses 'ex-centric', it is not so in absolute terms. The shifting field of relations wherein experience is constituted, is stabilised by human embodiment, and the standpoint of free agency. These two factors coincide in rational insights and decision-making. What is fundamental is not this or that moment of self-consciousness, but the urge to create or discover meaning that is embodied in every such moment. It is this primal urge into meaning which is made vivid in the experience of the sublime. The best art of postmodern times, therefore, restores some notion of an authentic self which is admittedly more complex than hitherto admitted, but which cannot be analysed away in a mere play of relations. On these terms, if properly understood and explained, sublime art has the capacity to rehumanise.

Notes

1 Walter Benjamin, *Illuminations*, trans. H Zohn, Verso, London, 1983.

2 Jean Baudrillard, *Simulations*, trans. Foss, Patton and Beitchmann, Semiotext, New York, 1983, p41.

3 See for example, Part Two of my *Critical Aesthetics and Postmodernism*, The Clarendon Press, Oxford, 1993.

4 Edmund Burke, *A Philosophical Inquiry into the Origin of Our Ideas of the Sublime and the Beautiful*, ed.

John Boulton, Routledge Kegan Paul, London, 1958, p136.

5 For a critical exposition see Chapter 4 to 7 of my *The Kantian Sublime: From Morality to Art*, Clarendon Press, Oxford, 1989.

6 *ibid*, Chapter 7.

7 Quoted in Jonathan Watkins's introduction to Parker's contribution to a group exhibition, *Austellunghaus im Grassmuseum Leipzig*, 1993.

Cornelia Parker, Neither From Nor Towards, *1992, suspended bricks washed into pebbles by the sea and collected from the beach at the foot of the cliffs*

THE SUBLIME IS HOW
PHILIP TAAFFE AND WILL BARNET
Cliff McMahon

Barnett Newman wrote a famous article 'The Sublime is Now' for the journal *Tiger's Eye* in 1945. In it, Newman indicated that he had pondered the classical literature of the sublime, and concluded that 'modern artists are struggling to regain a genuine sublime subject in an age devoid of efficacious sublime myth, and that these painters reassert the desire for the exaltation of the sublime by making the sacred cathedral zone out of ourselves, out of our own feeling'.[1] Since sublimity is a mode of reality and of human experience, it is the 'how' of a painting which carries the seal and modality of the sublime. It should be illuminating to consider the presence of the sublime in the paintings of Philip Taaffe and Will Barnet, one abstract and the other figural, one touched by negativity and one fully positive.

Taaffe's concern for the sublime is not disputable. It was appropriate to open this article with a reference to Newman's 'The Sublime is Now', because Taaffe has published a statement (as part of a symposium) on the value of Newman's essay. Taaffe judges that when Newman rejects previous rhetoric of the sublime and turns away from the beautiful to his own sense of the sublime, 'what Newman really does in his essay is to present the case for a negative sublime. This is a sublime of disassociation, a Great Refusal of the Sublime. His ambition was the realisation of a raw frontier which would break the stranglehold of the rhetoric of exaltation. He wanted to sail across an ocean of sheer terrifying potentiality . . . He would clear away these impediments of history through his practice of a negative sublime. However, in spite of the enormous goal of "making cathedrals out of our feelings", Newman could not have failed to realise that he was also in the process of inventing a new rhetoric of exaltation'.[2] Taaffe is certainly correct about Newman having created a new sublime rhetoric, and this suggests that on the basis of considerable negativity, Newman reached his own positive sublime. Taaffe is not correct in limiting Newman to 'sheer terrifying potentiality' (which would be a negative state) because Newman offered a number of positive concepts that reached beyond the merely potential. In exactly what sense, then, may we follow Taaffe's logic and locate elements of negativity in Newman's programme? Several items seem clear:

(1) Newman's sense of a modern spiritual condition deprived of all traditional sublime myth; (2) Newman's rejection of previous rhetoric of the sublime in favour of a raw new existential grounding; (3) Newman's sense of disassociation deriving from points one and two; (4) Newman's warfare against the past efforts to attain a sublime of formal beauty rather than rugged strength; and (5) Newman's grounding of the sublime not in external reality but in strong subjective feelings. Kant of course also grounded the sublime in subjectivity, but valorised reason rather than strong emotion. It was probably Burke's stress on strong emotion that caused Newman (in his essay) to favour Burke over other theorists.

Taaffe goes on to make other important points. He writes: 'Now the sublime, surely we must all realise, is an experience essential to the preservation of our humanity. Especially . . . since we are living in a sublimity-deprived society. Yes, I favour the ascendancy of a sublime art'. After adding that we should not rule out beauty as part of the sublime because 'any beautiful result can only be the outcome of our aspirations for sublimity', Taaffe declares, 'we will take any rhetoric of exaltation and do with it as we see fit. We will construct a mock-sublime to summon the sublime by indirection, because teasing or entertaining the sublime is just another way of aspiring towards sublimity. I'm interested in a sublimity which encourages laughter and delight in the face of profound uncertainty. And, finally, I do not care to argue against the possible coexistence of the sublime and beautiful if it can be envisioned as a terrible and awesome synthesis'.[3] Thus Taaffe encourages analysts of his paintings to be alert for a mock sublime, for a sense of joy rising above 'profound uncertainty', and for combinations of beauty and sublimity.

Taaffe's own statements offer a second region of interest which has sublime potential: the concept of a particular sacred set. In a 1987 interview Taaffe declared: 'I often think of the issues of Modernism in theological terms. Theology extracts an exegesis or makes a story from a number of sacred, inspired or supernatural events. In doing so, these sacred events become amplified, more lucid, more approachable. Perhaps we should see Modernism as a field of inquiry in that sense; as a series of inspired

Will Barnet, Edge of the World, *1979, oil on canvas*

moments, as a theological history to be examined and made lucid'.[4] Taaffe adds that 'Modernism consisted of a series of artistic events in conflict which superseded one another. The key attribute of the postmodern condition is the inability to make a new rupture'.[5] Yet the contemporary artists, if they cannot rupture, can integrate the present and past in a 'syncretism' involving 'accretions of cultural artefacts brought together in ways that suggest unification rather than dissolution or disjunction'. This syncretism is an effort 'to take all those violent and inflammatory artistic movements and give them new breath, to allow the consciousness of our moment to reshape them. This is what we have to do: to incorporate as much knowledge and awareness as possible into our work'.[6] I will argue later that this Taaffe project is itself a sublime task.

Taaffe next describes a crucial element in his painterly method: the essential idea and pictorial frame of the painting is ruthlessly determined ahead of time on rational, logical grounds (not any intuitive emergence) and 'the painting then becomes a way of amplifying or negating that structure'. This method sounds fairly formalist, yet Taaffe asserts that 'my work has a formal element to it, but it is not formalist . . . I am more interested in physical, expressive, compulsive and psychological ingredients beyond formalism, a search for a ruthless thing. I am not interested in making a pretty object. It has to be ruthless'.[7]

Taaffe's sense of the sacred moments in modernism is especially saturated with what he recognises as his deep liking for the colour-field abstract expressionists. He names Kenneth Noland and Ellsworth Kelly as painters whose vision is layered into his work as he tries to 'fuse' his 'sensibility' with his predecessors. Taaffe declares 'I am really in love with the New York School, with Clyfford Still, Mark Rothko, Ad Reinhardt and Barnett Newman. For me, they were crucial'.[8] Thus for Taaffe, the sacred events of artistic Modernism will turn on the first and second generation of Abstract Expressionism, the first generation having shared a strong sense of a sublime subject. And contrary to what some art historians claim, Noland and Kelly communicate a high, austere, and noble idealism that transcends formalism and decorative value.

Pointing to his sublime subject, Taaffe (as would Barnet) declares, 'we need profoundly ceremonial and ethical works in our midst right now; we don't need formal paintings. We need something which has history pouring out of it, which has grandeur of scale but which is also specific and starkly detailed'.[9] He adds that while he has a romantic streak, plus minimalist tendencies, he guards against romanticism by truthfulness to 'external reality',

and avoids the simplistic effects that might accompany minimalism: 'I want my paintings to be complex and subtly expressive . . . to make something which puts the viewer outside of himself in an ecstatic interplay, in *ekstasis*', and paintings should be complex enough to 'subvert expectations'.[10] Obviously Taaffe is seeking his own sublime subject in a ceremonial and ethical art that takes the viewer to an impersonal *ekstasis*: delivers a challenge, a jolt of subversion, a complexity attractive to intellect; and seeks grandeur in scale.

Taaffe, quite correctly understanding the 20th century as an age of criticism, notes that his theodicy of inspired moments in art history 'enables a criticality to develop, and gives us some sense of direction', and notes that the New Abstraction he speaks for 'has been called cynical, but it is not'.[11] If it were strongly cynical, there would be no elevation to the sublime. It should be stressed that Taaffe's New Abstraction might well be called a New Abstract Rationalism, with its logically predetermined forms and logical historical syncretism. It is new in the greater place given to difficulty, to comic irony, and to critical alertness – as if touched by the spirit of Duchamp, and yet grafting the Duchamp manner onto a more coherent historical programme. Has Duchamp been merged with Abstract Expressionism in order to treat modern and postmodern habits of mind? In any case, this critical rationalism in Taaffe may suggest that he reins in the romantic imagination and draws closer to Kant's theory of the sublime wherein the saving principle is reason.[12]

Additional remarks from Taaffe are given in a kind of fake symposium which Dan Cameron pieces together from separate interviews as an introduction to his *NY Art Now*. In Taaffe's segments the painter declares that his theodicy of Modernism requires that artists 'bring back the sacred and the inspired to serve our present needs'.[13] He sharply reveals his own moral instrumentalism: 'The painting should say that there's another possible world by saying, "Look at the world inside this painting, and figure out how the two can come together". That should be the level of intellectual engagement that a painting sets up. One's appreciation of the world inside the painting should produce a more acute awareness of life'.[14] If this is not strong enough, Taaffe continues insisting that artists must present a vision 'for some kind of paradisical situation on earth', hoping their works will influence persons of power to change life from a 'humanistic perspective'.[15] Finally, he insists that modern faith is a vital category: 'It's important to determine the ways in which our belief has failed us. How are we to re-channel our miscast belief? How do we make

Will Barnet, Reclining Woman, *1978, oil on canvas*

the leap from modernist faith to a faith in what has supplanted Modernism?'[16]

Michael Kohn has published an interview with Taaffe which focused on the painter's reworking of Op art. Taaffe declares that his intent is to re-identify Op art so that by adding a strongly personal element, the icon is 'transformed in such a way that it becomes something else entirely' and is 'subverted by the possibility of being personal'. This subjective lyrical assertion keeps Taaffe close to the founders of Abstract Expressionism. Taaffe adds that when he manifests surrealist content he intends to inform it 'by minimalism and conceptual art', to enlarge its range, to postulate a larger freedom, to demonstrate 'that today anything is possible, and can be assimilated'.[17] After observing that in his newest work he is 'staining the cloth background very minutely, close to Rothko', Taaffe concludes the interview by further explaining his sense of enlarged freedom, his programme to bridge over 'an invisibility that comes between a previous historical visibility and what we are now doing', a project 'that can have the possibility of extending our knowledge'.[18]

We do not yet have much insightful literature on Taaffe, but some interesting articles have appeared. Dan Cameron has seen in Taaffe a 'large-scale . . . no-punches pulled, transcendental abstraction', yet he thinks the mystical tones in Taaffe are undercut by a touch of the absurd. However, Cameron's point cannot be accepted because Taaffe's call for ethical and sublime subjects and modes is too clear. Cameron is right, however, when he adds that in the 'transcendental abstraction' of Taaffe, 'the art isn't in what you're seeing – it's what's been awakened inside of you'.[19] In general, Cameron is not in touch with Taaffe's deepest aims. Seth Edenbaum develops the thesis that there is a set of painters (Duchamp, Warhol, Koons, Nagy, Prince, Taaffe, Salle) who live in an anti-idealist, isolated, cerebral state and must parody Modernism because they cannot accept it: 'they do not accept idealist order, nor do they transcend it. The art of high Modernism is idealist, monotheistic, and Apollonian. To change this, or to adapt to change . . . [they] could have moved towards a more polymarphous form. They chose not to, instead adopting a strange hybrid of idealist structure, an anti-idealism or anti-theology (a peversion), and simultaneously a warped objectivity toward their chosen form'.[20] Edenbaum is representative of a current deep-rooted critical tendency to create overly melodramatic conflicts, a kind of will to conflict. His thesis may apply to some of his set of painters, but not to Duchamp or Taaffe. Edenbaum ignores Duchamp's frequently iterated idealism

about the regal sovereignty of the intellect and ignores Taaffe's celebration of ritualised Modernism that goes along with the artist's rather gentle sense of parody. Also, Edenbaum ignores the fact that the giants of high Modernism such as Joyce, Eliot and Wallace Stevens were remarkably isolated and private, and were brilliant parodists. Edenbaum, Cameron, and other interpreters must pay close attention to Taaffe's own statements.

G Roger Denson has offered an article on Taaffe's reworkings of Islamic art motifs. While criticising Taaffe for projecting some improper Westernised and Platonised perspectives on Islam, Denson also calls attention to Taaffe's important goal: moving beyond nationalism to ponder, through his art images, the root Islamic concept of cosmic unity emanating from Godhead, a unity conveyed by the abstract geometrical patterns in Islamic art, and grounded in the Pythagorean sense of basic geometric forms as the foundation of all created things.[21] Denson notes that Islam, leaning on Pythagorean cosmology, takes a single point for the cosmic centre and origin of all forms; such a point being the centre for iconic circles which can symbolise cosmic harmony, in that the eternal Platonic circle contains the geometric forms of the triangle, square, and hexagon, and can also symbolise perfect justice and equality.[22] Denson might have added that the Pythagoreans were the first intellects to postulate a primary particle (a single point), and that God can create forms of matter if He can count to four, going from point to line to triangle to pyramid. Denson concludes by connecting Taaffe's use of Islamic forms to Piaget's theory of creative assimilation between past forms and new data, an assimilation promising ongoing enlargements in zones of freedom. Denson correctly declares that these adventurous projects of Taaffe mock the overly cynical and melodramatic view of 'the end of originality'.[23]

From these comments by Taaffe and others, various elements in Taaffe's programme are noteworthy: the reanimating of the sublime vision of Rothko, Newman, Still and other Abstract Expressionists; the freedom to retain past rhetoric of the sublime; the search for the sublime in the current state of diminished idealism; the creation of a mock-sublime rising joyously from uncertainty; the conception of Modernism as a theodicy of sacred events; a strong ruthless rationalism; the need for ceremonial and ethical works on a grand scale; strategies with a shock of subversion; a fruitful paradise vision; a sense of a Kantian dynamical sublime in the energy and power of art to change the world; the subversion of Op art by injecting it with lyrical subjectivity; the assimilation of classical Islamic icons of Pythagorean religiosity into contemporary abstract forms; the incorporation of most of these various purposes into a general strategy of bridging the invisible zone between a past triumph of art and a contemporary sensibility; the rootedness of these purposes in the infinite freedom of the artist to assimilate from the entire museum without walls, whether primitive, Western, or Eastern; and the search for a viable new faith along with exposing why past faith has failed. This last item might seem vague, but as a possible example, Taaffe's strong allegiance to abstraction carries with it a strong rejection of anecdote, and most of the major religions lean heavily on anecdote without realising its sentimental and pernicious effect. An eternal thing is contaminated by a localised popular story. An abstract idea and an abstract painting can avoid the contamination of the local and contingent. Of course, figural art properly handled (as in the case of Barnet) can also undermine anecdote.

Since Taaffe clearly appreciates and employs a negative sublime with ironic flavour, his position may be illuminated by a work which stresses the negative sublime, *The Romantic Sublime* by Thomas Weiskel. Although Weiskel is often vague and contradictory, and leaves loose ends, he does stake out important ground in theory of the sublime, and some of his insights can be applied to Taaffe. Weiskel declares that 'the essential claim of the sublime is that man can, in feeling and in speech, transcend the human. What, if anything, lies beyond the human-God or the gods, the demon or Nature, is a matter for great disagreement'.[24] Using this logic, Weiskel concludes that 'a humanistic sublime is an oxymoron', adding that as the idea of a divine presence recedes, any sense of the sublime would become problematic and 'the secondary or problematic sublime is pervaded by the nostalgia and the uncertainty of minds involuntarily secular'.[25] In passing, we should note that Weiskel is not quite correct. The sublime requires a jolt to the intellect followed by a transcendent resolution that is an exaltation; yet this formula can be fully humanistic. The necessary transcendent zone could come from a Kantian transcendental ego, a Kantian sense of the essence of the vocation of mankind, a set of Platonic forms, a set of universal laws, a theory of history, a sense of Nietzsche's superman, a sense of the Major Man of Wallace Stevens, a set of universal Jungian archetypes and so on. Weiskel is right to this extent: a richer and more productive life for sublime encounters will be manifested if the upward move to transcendence can be invested with a sense of the holy and sacred. Of course the holy and sacred

could be redistributed so as to avoid a supernatural being, if anyone could make a persuasive case.

Weiskel believes that the Romantic sublime was 'a massive transposition of transcendence into a naturalistic key; in short, a stunning metaphor'.[26] Weiskel does not try to specify the metaphor. It would have to be something like 'the world as paradise' or 'natural supernaturalism' or 'the poetic imagination as redeemer'. Since Weiskel actually tries to describe a sense of the sublime to replace the outmoded Romantic paradigm, one would think that he would not call his text *The Romantic Sublime*. His explanation is that the mind-set of the 20th century is typically seen as 'a late variant of Romanticism'; therefore 'whatever structure we find behind the Romantic sublime should still be in place'.[27] In passing, it is worth noting that Romanticism was sharply condemned by 20th-century giants such as Eliot, Joyce, Wallace Stevens, Hart Crane, and Robert Frost (as well as Nietzsche). Weiskel claims that our age cannot accept the Romantic sublime and its correlative idealism because our age is too ironic: 'To please us, the sublime must now be abridged, reduced and parodied as the grotesque, somehow hedged with irony to assure us we are not imaginative adolescents'.[28]

Weiskel's basic aim is to use psychological terms to find the deepest core structure of any sublime experience, to find 'a structure beneath the vast epiphenomenon of the sublime', the structure of 'the sublime original moment – in which a burden . . . is lifted and there is an influx of power'.[29] Weiskel, showing some uneasiness about his project, adds that 'it is difficult to be wholly clear about the logical status of the metaphorical moment we seek'.[30] Part of the problem is that he seeks an essentialism and a foundationalism while trying to show an allegiance to postmodem thought which rejects both. Also, Weiskel observes that even if we locate an upward thrust via metaphor, we should not take the metaphor too literally, but try to hark back to a 'moment of origin, an instant before the metaphor crystallised'.[31]

To move away from Kantian idealism, Weiskel hopes to 'preserve the dichotomous structure of Kant's formulation in a "realist" or psychological account', an account in which 'the metaphorical moment of the sublime would be understood as an internalisation or sublimation of the imagination's relation to the object'.[32] Weiskel believes we need a de-idealised psychological theory because 'many also experience the sublime whose adhesion to the empirical is firm to the point of scepticism toward any particular transcendent scheme'.[33] According to Weiskel the contemporary sensibility requires a reduced sublime because 'the presentation of

unattainability is phenomenologically a negation, a falling away from what might be seized, perceived, known', and thus there is 'an abridgement of the sublime moment so that we are confined to the second phase and await futilely the restorative reaction which never comes, except ironically', and for this the 'wasteland' metaphor is appropriate.[34] This bleak passage seems to contradict Weiskel's earlier claim that in a sublime experience there must be a resolution and an influx of power.

In a not too clear section, Weiskel argues that the necessary shock or disruption can arise when some signifier is overloaded, or when some sense of meaning (a signified) is overloaded. Since these two modes are phenomenological and not idealistic, Weiskel can add that 'this modal dichotomy proves to be far more interesting and useful than a thematic opposition of naturalised versus idealist or other classificatory schemes'.[35] Weiskel observes that to bridge over the first mode, when some signifier is overloaded, a metaphor is required; while to bridge in the second mode of overloaded meaning, the device of metonymy is better, a metonymous form being one that acts like a pictured substitute, and not like the identification of metaphor.[36] Weiskel adds that he will treat the metonymy mode as positive and the metaphor mode as negative, though he does not justify this decision.[37] Weiskel has in general used metaphor in talking about the reduced modern sceptical sublime. He uses the term 'sublimation' to mean a displacement or substitution, and admits that his ideas must be tentative because so far there is no full psychological theory of sublimation.[38] Predictably, Weiskel connects his secularised, materialistic, and psychological view to Freudian psychology, which he admits is also vague.[39] With his Freudian ego model, he declares that when an artist tries to reproduce the sublime experience through an art object, this entails a loss of freedom for the ego.[40] We may take this as a further irony.

Since the realm of signified meanings is also the realm of ideology, Weiskel proposes that when the mind in the sublime encounter makes its move to restore balance, the move may be dictated by some prevailing ideology by some ulterior motive, as in the case of Kant's desire to enhance reason. If ideology holds the key, then the transcendental turn should be viewed as a fiction.[41] Kant would respond that the turn to reason is a phenomenon, and not a fiction. Weiskel believes it is a fiction, which justifies throwing out Kant's ideology of a return to reason and replacing it with a concept like 'repressed traumata'. Weiskel thinks we can argue about the content of the higher zone, but must keep some sense of the real existence of an 'invisible world'.[42] Weiskel slides in one of his few efforts to name the essence of the sublime: 'that sudden turning of the mind in an awe-full intuition'.[43] The sublime event 'does not risk quietism' and 'splits consciousness into alienated halves'.[44]

Weiskel takes note of William Blake's view that the authentic sublime is not idealistic or murky, but is carried cleanly in concrete particulars.[45] But Weiskel does not do anything with Blake's unique position. He notes that 'the negative sublime begins with an excessive interest in nature, and ends with an excessive disdain of nature' when reason and idealism take over.[46] And 'unlike the positive sublime, whose ultimate form is repetitive and circular, the negative sublime theoretically aims toward a unique disillusionment – the unmasking of the "subreption" by which an object seems sublime'.[47] In other words, the positive sublime accomplishes a fully harmonious reconciliation of conflicts, while the negative sublime maintains a sense of conflict and sabotage, which is what Weiskel means, but cannot state very clearly. Since the positive sublime locates the ego in a smooth world of harmony, Weiskel relates it to Wordsworth and calls it the egotistical sublime, in contrast to the negative Freudian sublime which postulates a conflict between the split forces, which can all be encompassed under the idea of the Oedipal conflict of father and son.[48] Weiskel tries to catch Burke in the Oedipal pattern by suggesting that the danger and terror stressed by the latter could be related to 'an unconscious fantasy of parricide'.[49] Summarising this Freudian direction, he concludes that 'the sublime moment recapitulates and thereby establishes the Oedipus complex, whose positive resolution is the basis of culture itself'.[50] Weiskel is perceptive enough not to push his Oedipal element too far, his final position being that even deeper than the Oedipal conflict there is a more primitive mechanism of attraction and repulsion, and behind this an even more elemental wish 'to be pleasurably stimulated'.[51]

Weiskel argues that in the positive or egotistical sublime, the higher value zone is immanent rather than transcendent, because the sublime dialectic comes to rest in the self and avoids dramatic trauma; however because the concept of self is now seen as problematic, as an 'unresolved ambivalence', the 'structure of the egotistical sublime ends precisely at the point of ambivalence in which we found the beginnings of the negative Sublime'.[52]

Weiskel did not finish his manuscript, and thus his rather rambling speculations are never brought into a clear and coherent synthesis. His main point, however, is relevant to a reading of Taaffe: the thesis that our Modern and somewhat postmodern

Will Barnet, Introspection, 1980, oil on canvas

age requires a negative sublime which must somehow reach a tentative resolution that maintains tension and conflict and rests in a sense of irony, plus the thesis that a structure for a genuine sublime continues to exist in the deepest psychological ground, even if the modern mind is dubious about higher zones of reality. Weiskel's ideas come close to Taaffe also in view of Taaffe's previously noted aim to move beyond formalism to a ruthless construct which encompasses 'physical, expressive, compulsive and psychological ingredients'. Weiskel's whole study tries to lay a framework for the mechanisms of the sublime which are rooted in a compulsive psychology of primal desire and Freudian psychic conflict. Quite a number of Weiskel's descriptions of our contemporary spiritual state (necessitating a negative sublime) are applicable to Taaffe: uncertainty about the needed higher world; residues of Romanticism; a reduced and parodied sublime related to the withdrawal of the gods; the uses of metaphor or metonymy to generate a sublime resolution; overloads in things or meanings; the compulsions of Freudian psychology; the retention of some elements of negation and conflict in a postmodern sublime; and the search for deepest origins in the most primitive psychic mechanisms of desire and pleasure.[53]

The theory of the negative sublime is also enriched by Louis Wirth Marvik's study of Mallarmé. Wirth emphasises that the Kantian model can be viewed in this sense: 'the subject's enthusiasm for the absolute, that is the theme of a given representation, must be tempered by the ironical perception of the representation's shortcomings'; and 'the sublime, as Kant showed, is a negative experience, in which the subject, obedient to the dictates of his moral attitude, voluntarily immolates his imagination to his reason, and his pleasure in the real world to his respect for a principle of unreal perfection'.[54] While Kant's conception of the sublime is not this negative, his model could be useful in creating a contemporary sublime which contains an ironic recognition that the sublime calls mankind upwards, yet does not allow a full realisation of harmony, paradise or the outer mystery. Mallarmé and Taaffe, amongst others could be interpreted in this mixed positive and negative mode. Speaking broadly, Taaffe's ironic negative sublime should be suspected in his subversions of aesthetic attitudes which limit full artistic freedom; his sense of a diminished contemporary idealism; his mockery of faith which failed; his use of a paradise vision to undermine and convert the powers and principalities of the commercial-political-pop world; and his own sublime vision as a rejection of contemporary scepticism and materialism.

Sublime possibilities in Taaffe's works may be augmented by citing several items from the classical literature of the sublime. Longinus declared that among major sources of the sublime, the foremost is 'the faculty of grasping great conceptions', and that often a bare idea can reach the sublime when 'the thought is very great'.[55] Taaffe's keel principle of holding the sacred moments of modern art in a constantly renewed synthesis in the mode of a theodicy qualifies as a conception which reaches sublimity. Additionally, when Longinus locates a calm and reasoned sublime narrative in the history works of Thucydides,[56] Longinus assumes that historical forces may carry sublimity, a concept relevant to Taaffe's effort to absorb Abstract Expressionism as a strong historical force. Any strong force would fall under Kant's conception of the dynamical sublime. Longinus also declares that serial repetition may generate a sublime experience.[57] Serial repetition seems to hint of the limitless and the infinite, which would fall under Kant's mathematical sublime. It may well be that such a mystical sense lies behind Taaffe's Untitled 1984, a powerful Venetian blind working of elegant, high-tech, torpedo serial shapes, touched by spirituality in the whisper tones of pale yellow, pale lavender, and pale blue. In this work, another principle of Longinus may suggest sublime content: that the sublime may be conveyed by leaps from the one to the many.[58] Certainly the motif of one and many constitutes the structural frame of this work. All abstract painters enjoy a certain advantage in treating the sublime, since rejecting natural forms in favour of abstract ones supplies an immediate ascent towards the spiritual, intellectual, and ineffable. To abstract is in a sense to elevate, and there is an inherent grandeur in the abstract mode. Longinus, like Kant, holds that the subjective intellectual and spiritual realm offers more range for the sublime than the physical universe does.[59]

Longinus also notes that intense emotions are a source of the sublime and that emotional intensity can be heightened by the push of question and answer exchanges.[60] Obviously in Taaffe's We are Not Afraid there is a question and answer exchange with Newman's Who's Afraid of Red, Yellow and Blue series. Additionally, Longinus points out that a sublime effect is generated when the past is thrust into the present,[61] which Taaffe accomplishes in his general programme of reconstituting the sacred history of Abstract Expressionism and assimilating values from past art splendours, such as Islamic art. In broad terms of the ontology and psychology of the sublime, the sudden thrust of past into present would constitute a jolt from the surprising meeting of conflicting realms, a jolt in which terms of reason such as 'past' and 'present' would cover complex, difficult, rugged terrain which could not be caught in any easy harmonious act of understanding or in any single aesthetic image. In such clashes there will be some murky and ineffable edges which increase the sublime content. In my opinion, since we all daily thrust the past into the present, this mundane happening sheds light on a brief and enigmatic comment by Kant that the sublime rests upon deep-seated habitual patterns in the everyday life of all people.[62]

The prevailing darkness and fuzzy edges of Taaffe's Untitled 1984 may be connected to Edmund Burke's claim that the sublime is enhanced by darkness and obscurity. The powerful serial repetition of the work is illuminated by Burke's observation that sublime things 'make some sort of approach towards infinity'[63] – which is what Longinus had in mind. Burke also connects the sublime to states of emptiness, privation, and solitude.[64]

Logically, since the sublime activates an upward turning, Burke claims that verticals are more sublime than horizontals.[65] Taaffe often uses strong verticals, as in the Newman-like white zips in Untitled 1984, and in the wholly vertical Color Field Painting, and also in the columns and zips of We Are Not Afraid. Another effective work, Taaffe's There, Now, 1985, is 78 inches high and 12 inches wide. It contains two slender ascending black bars divided by a faintly stippled white bar which shades towards pale yellow and lavender at the bottom. The striking, soaring effect is rendered richer because Taaffe is creating a dialogue with Newman's sculptures Here I, Here II, and Here III, which feature slender dark rods ascending from a more or less roughened base.[66] It might seem to be pushing sublimity too much in making such connections, yet they are plausible because we know that Taaffe is seeking a contemporary ground for the sublime and we know that he has absorbed the sublime dimensions of such predecessors as Rothko, Newman, and Still. Using Taaffe's logic, There, Now could be a direct Newmanesque raising of the sublime from a raw concrete existential base, or if there is irony, then we meet an indirect negative sublime to be added to the general cultural negativity of the existential position, and the irony might well imply too much narrowness of range for Newman.

In a very important passage, Burke notes that any great difficulty can reach the sublime. So far it has not been sufficiently emphasised that abstract art offers, usually, a challenge of great difficulty to its viewers as they struggle (and are taught) to make the sudden leaps from abstract icon to metaphysical meaning. The difficulty index in abstract art finds a companion zone in the literary difficulty of modernist giants such as Joyce, Stevens, Eliot, Yeats, Hopkins, Hart Crane, and Faulkner, and a further companion in the difficulties of scientific and mathematical theory. In the case of painters like Taaffe, the difficulty becomes interestingly elevated when we must consider the juxtaposition between a complex assimilation of past aesthetic programmes and a fresh sublime vision, along with a mock-heroic indirect implication of a contemporary negative sublime. The mixing of positive and negative currents should be seen as a promising sublime strategy. In a sense, this is the pattern of Kant's sublime, when a negative impasse is broken by a positive resolution. Burke offers this valuable passage on the sublimity of what is difficult: 'When any work seems to have required immense force and labor to effect it'.[67]

Additionally (and relevant to a number of past and present painters), Burke observes that sublime aims in painting are enhanced by dark colours such as brown, black and deep purple, and in a remark that sheds light on Newman's Vir Heroicus Sublimis and other works, Burke states that while red is usually a cheerful colour, 'a strong red can carry sublimity'.[68] Taaffe's Color Field Painting is dominated by strong red, and is also conspicuous for seriality along with verticality. There seems to be no irony in this work, unless Taaffe is gently mocking excessive minimalism, when it is reduced to ornamentation.

Burke singles out not only light and darkness as sources of the sublime, but also all the colours revealed by light.[69] Obviously this principle would apply to all painting. What is involved here is the long mystical tradition of light in Western art, all the many connections between luminism, intellect, and soul, as this complex tradition has been enriched by painters and architects and also by biblical passages, religious festivals of light, Plato's Allegory of the Cave, the radiance of the Nous of Plotinus, and so on. The mystery and power of light, the way it is touched by absolute things, makes a common ground, for instance, between the Abstract Expressionists and figure painters such as Wyeth, whose recent Olga nudes (like works of Barnet) are about as mystical and sacramental as figural art can be. Burke adds the relevant point that mere coloured objects alone are not sufficient, there must also be some general context of intent appropriate to sublime aims.[70] This is obviously a crucial point, the proper reining in of a tendency to find the sublime everywhere. The sublime may be invoked only when there are plausible grounds – though this principle does not rule out a mode of sublimity for the mundane, if anyone can make the plausible case. Such a case would have to involve a concealed grandeur in the ordinary, a concept important to Barnet.

We may certainly assume that Taaffe's project to recover the sacred moments of Abstract Expressionism contains a strong moral imperative. Taaffe believes that contemporaries *ought* to make this effort to preserve the past, a preservation which serves the general public well. The connection between moral obligation and the sublime has been especially made by Kant. In one direction Kant argues that when reason supplies the needed unitary concept to resolve the jolt of a sublime encounter, this phenomenological event triggers our noble subjective awareness of the vocation of mankind as thinking rational and moral creatures.[71] In another direction Kant claims that each ethical self reaches its highest sublimity in its power to legislate universal moral laws binding on all rational people.[72] Such a power would touch infinity because it is an infinite power. While Moses may be seen as a supreme giver of moral laws, the truth is that the Ten Commandments were distillations out of normal life over a long period, and thus fit into Kant's model. On the spur of the moment, and in support of Kant, I might create two new universal laws: children must not be seriously frightened, and all colleges and universities should require courses in the history of philosophy, art, and music. I will mention only one of several of the additional ways by which Kant links aesthetics and morality. At one point Kant declares that aesthetic ideas found in beauty and sublimity protect mankind from boredom as they 'enliven the mind by opening out to it the prospect into an illimitable field of kindred representations'.[73]

These insights into the general social and moral value of art should be applied to Taaffe and other painters if one wants to do full justice to those moral vectors which lace through all works of art and which create part of the aura of the sublime.

Nietzsche's theory of the sublime is also relevant to an assessment of Taaffe. Nietzsche construed all great projects which shape culture and thought as artistic projects. For Nietzsche, artistic creation is the only actor on the human stage, and he sees scientists and religious leaders as artists. For Nietzsche the sublime is reached when artistic symbols ward off and protect against the horrors and absurdities of the cruel Dionysiac state of nature. These horrors and absurdities are not acceptable to the human spirit, not acceptable to the will to power which demands joy and triumph. Here is Nietzsche's crucial remark: 'Art approaches, as a saving and healing enchantress; she alone is able to transform these nauseating reflections on the awfulness or absurdity of existence into representations wherewith it is possible to live; these are the representations of the *sublime* as the artistic subjugation of the awful, and the *comic* as the artistic delivery from the nausea of the absurd'.[74] Obviously for Nietzsche, the entire project of the artist becomes the sublime endeavour, and the sublime is attained when the symbolic representations of art generate some elevated vision of joy, meaning, value and purpose, such that a culture can transcend the negative horrors of existence and dwell in a world of saving fictions created by major artists. Nietzsche's theory allows us to suggest that Taaffe's general project carries enough metaphysical idealism to be a sublime project.

Lyotard has located the entire honour of art in its continuation of a transcendental sublime vision, and Gadamer has declared that art in general reveals a holy and whole sense of the world and mankind's 'finitude before that which transcends him'; that art may be 'the only way granted to us finite beings to relate to what we call eternity'; that all human experience must be liberated from contingency and 'raised into ideality'; and that each art work is itself the shock that triggers the imaginative intuition of the sublime.[75] Consequently, theorists of the sublime have considerable latitude and warrant for following the Nietzschean model and equating the ontology of art with the ontology of the sublime. Of course if some art works have no such exalted aim, they would lack sublimity, unless the lack itself constitutes an indirect recognition, a secondary sublime.

None of these searchings into classical theory of the sublime are much help in clearly resolving one of the chief problems presented by Taaffe. Suppose that his *We Are Not Afraid* constitutes in part a tribute to Newman's colour-field search for an existential sublime and yet also contains an ironic note of parody – as if Taaffe perhaps has better things to be afraid of. At the moment, we do not know enough about Taaffe to declare clearly and confidently just how his positive and negative elements are pictorially asserted, but we are learning. Obviously Taaffe's construction of a theodicy for Abstract Expressionism informs works such as *There, Now, Color Field Painting* and *We Are Not Afraid*. Even if Taaffe thinks we know more than the past, he agrees with Eliot that the past is what we know. These works exemplify also his general concept of bridging from present to past by a complex assimilation, potentially a sublime project due to idealism, difficulty, and the thrusting of past into present. The Moorish Islamic assimilation is strongly conveyed by Taaffe's *Rosette*, 1987. The

Mediterranean arabesques testify to the iconic geometric purity by which Islam protects Godhead from temporal and human contamination. The observer's gaze is drawn powerfully to the white radiance at the centre, as if to Eliot's still point in *Four Quartets*. Taaffe's use of the numinous white, plus all the colours of the solar spectrum, connects to Burke's designation of light and the colours vivified by light as one mode of the sublime. The sense of Platonic and Pythagorean cosmic harmony in this work is powerful. Taaffe's search for beauty is sublimely serious – he should be praised for the chain of blue and green circles on a red field in *Rosette*, by which he boldly and effectively cross-fertilises the soul of Islam with the spirit of Abstract Expressionism from Mondrian to the present.

The iconic power of the circle is also presented in Taaffe's *Big Iris*, 1986. We might view this as a move toward Islamic circularity and seriality, but even without such a component, we would still see the one and many motifs, plus the subverting of the surface superficiality of Op art by using its forms to declare both a subjective lyricism and a metaphysical elevation. We would see ornamentation raised to intellection. Almost the same may be said of Taaffe's *Overtone*, 1983, wherein an ostensible Op art form is shot through with lyrical colourations that break the too simple Op format, with the denser concentration of lyric variations in the lower half forcing a kind of classical easel reading onto the subverted Op form. Works like *Overtone*, *Big Iris*, and *We Are Not Afraid* reveal the sense of humour and joy that Taaffe mentioned as an ongoing source of the sublime in an age that claims (wrongly) to have little to sing about, little to invest with transcendence. For all of Taaffe's works, we should keep in mind his belief that any conspicuous beauty in painting is an 'outcome of our aspirations for sublimity', a principle which Barnet would heartily endorse.

Certainly Will Barnet in his latest phase offers a sharp contrast to Taaffe in his more fully positive conception of a sublime subject. A number of the previously noted resources for the sublime apply to Barnet: greatness of conception, the sublimity of historical forces, hints of the one and many, the thrusting of past into present, darkness for depth and radiance for height, strong verticals, the colour domination of black and purple, ethical seriousness, a strong transcendentalism and a strong sense of the sacred as advocated by Lyotard and Gadamer, and a general symbolic programme with the sublime value of a Nietzschean project. Perpetuating the grand idealism of Modernism (and in a positive mode different from the ironically stained sensibility of Taaffe) Barnet shares with Taaffe a

rejection of contemporary scepticism, bleakness and materialism. A group of Barnet's own comments provides valuable insights. Like Taaffe, Barnet has worked out a theodicy of sacred moments from the past, but his chosen set is the whole of art history. Avis Berman offers Barnet's statement: 'The only real competition is with artists throughout the centuries. And it has to start from the very beginning. Otherwise you don't have the roots to work with. Throughout your career you're constantly evaluating yourself against people you feel are ancestral figures . . . You discuss ideas with your contemporaries, but your ultimate discourse is with the masters'.[76] Obviously the past which Barnet thrusts into the present is the museum without walls of Malraux. Among the set of ancestral figures that Barnet and various interpreters list as important to the painter are classical Greek vase painters, Cimabue, Giotto, Botticelli, the Renaissance painters in general, Poussin, Rembrandt, Daumier, Vermeer, Velázquez, Cezanne, Picasso, Matisse, Leger, Seurat, Modigliani, Gris, and oriental wood-block masters. This list points to several values: abstractions from the real in the interest of idealism; reduction; flatness and frontality; the nobility in people; formalism; beauty, serenity and harmony; and domesticity. Of his interest in the family motif Barnet declares: 'The family unit is the essence of civilisation; everything is based on it. During the Renaissance many of the paintings were of family groups and their ceremonies – the vision of the family reflects the history of art'.[77] Barnet tilts his mundane family scenes towards the sublime in his crucial remark given by Caril Dreyfuss McHugh: 'An everyday event is a tremendous thing. I want the everydayness to be exciting. It becomes a symbol, an abstraction'. In short, the overt mundane burns with a covert fire, and in Barnet's works this makes for a subreption. McHugh also gives the painter's observation that he is 'trying to get at the grandeur in people, animals, birds'.[78]

Barnet's portraits, seemingly so austere, contain the kind of complexity and challenging difficulty that involve the sublime. He asserts that the essential traits of the sitter 'should be at the core of the work, but the painting must have other meanings – historical, environmental, psychological and formal'. His own family portraits are set in Maine, of which he writes: 'Maine, with its monumental primordial rocky coastline – its tall pine trees silhouetted against a vast luminous sky and ocean – its deep harbors and ancient piers, caught my visual imagination. Added to this is Maine's transcendental history and its many myths, which stirred within me a depth of dramatic feeling and tension'.[79] In addition to this Friedrich-like sense of sky, ocean, and the mathematical sublime (which almost all interpreters stress), we should note the element that has been too much ignored: the long shadow of American transcendentalism with its own sublime vision in Melville, Emerson, Hawthorne, Thoreau, and Emily Dickinson.[80] The Friedrich tonality is clarified in a letter from Barnet: 'I was involved with the new problem of trying to deal with the sky, ocean and distances. I felt the need to come to grips with the radiant light found in the atmosphere without being realistic or literary. I want to dissociate from normal human activity the relationship between figure and nature, and to deal instead with the mysterious poetry of the two'.[81] A number of interpreters emphasise the intent of Barnet to create a timeless, Utopian, eternal region, obviously a sublime project.[82] Also, most interpreters highlight the cool and calm mode of Barnet. It is important to recall that Kant postulated a noble sublime, a calm and serene mental state at the polar opposite from the impassioned and rugged sublime. Kant declares that the cool sublime is higher than the hot, and he also names cool silent meditation as a possible sublime state (assuming profound meditation).[83] The whole of Barnet's latest work falls into the Kantian noble, meditative, rational sublime, and its infinite horizons are rich in the Kantian mathematical sublime.

In his full length study of Barnet (the best source for viewing Barnet's paintings), Robert Doty points to 'Barnet's penchant for mystical and symbolical overtones, for an art that transcends the ordinary'.[04] Doty emphasises 'stillness, and lucidity' in which 'a passing moment becomes an eternity',[85] and the Barnet women display a 'silent, eternal waiting', standing 'before an infinite horizon'.[86] Doty also locates the theme of 'the strength of the New England soul' in that 'the images of women and the sea are steeped in the spiritual values that nurtured the intellect of New England'.[87] Doty connects Barnet to the sublime of Mallarmé in the latter's 'attempt to recreate the world of man and nature as a Symbolist image of exquisite and near-abstract purity'.[88] In Barnet's 'female figure situated in a strange, haunting openness, immersed in unearthly light and atmosphere', Doty believes he is reaching for 'the outer limits of experience', an aim clearly fixed on the ineffable and transcendental sublime region.[89]

So far the interpreters have not made enough either of a tragic sense in Barnet's brooding women, or of the mythical shadow of the American transcendentalist thinkers and writers. Barnet's own set of sacred moments encompasses art history and the giants of modernist painting, but he has a special New England subset. In his strong, silent, intellectually brooding women we should see not just the fierce, isolated and confident individualism of Emerson and Thoreau, but also the powerful and intellectual Hester Prynne of *The Scarlet Letter*, as well as the powerful, secretive and enduring mind of Emily Dickinson. Barnet's women reveal intellect and are also charged with erotic mystery. Both Hester and Emily rose above deep tragedy, stormed the gates of heaven on their own metaphysical terms, and used their reason to contain an explosive eroticism. They both absorbed metaphysical probings at the axis of reality, which Melville admired in Hawthorne and immortalised in Captain Ahab. In Nietzsche's sense of a sublime project, carried by art symbols, Barnet's myth-centred project is sublime. Also, Barnet's noble and positive sublime is sufficiently many-layered as to deliver its own challenge and subreption to the viewer, demanding from him an alert ascent towards the comprehension of higher mysteries, thus reaching the sublime in the pattern declared by Lyotard and Gadamer. In assessing sublime effects in Barnet, we must remember that he broods upon the astonishment which belongs to the ostensibly mundane.

Barnet's *Reclining Woman*, 1978, offers a noble madonna elevation, the infinite ocean horizon, restrained eroticism in the female curves and phallic trees, the special interweaving of the poetry of both nature and woman, a strong verticality, a background of vast radiant light, and the sublime colours of black and purple. These same values inhere in *Edge of the World*, 1979, along with the high and austere New England mythology carried by the sea, the isolated brooding woman, and the severe rectangular New England architecture. There are sexual hints in the door, window, tree-trunks and female form, but the eroticism is disciplined. Barnet's silent women pondering pure minimal skies, infinite space, and infinite ocean invoke the Kantian noble sublime, in contrast to the turbulent New England ocean motifs of Winslow Homer. The sublime powers of black and purple speak forth in Barnet's *Dawn*, 1976-83 (as they do in Rothko's late work), and we have not seen a richer assimilation of portraiture, primitivism, Japanese woodblock elegance, and the cosmic simplified geometries of Platonic idealism (a syncretism Taaffe would admire). Barnet's *Early Morning* is a ritual celebration of the sacred in intellect, human craft, sky, ocean, eternity, and silence. Probably we should connect it not only to occidental luminism but also to Thoreau's *Walden*, a work overtly saturated with dawn symbolism and the worship of Aurora. Reinforcing all these features of his positive noble sublime, Barnet's *Introspection* adds favourite themes of a reading woman and white doves. The trees, doves, woman, tumbler, box and apple (closely akin to the concepts of inscape and instress in the poems of Gerard Manley Hopkins) cry out the seal of eternity upon their concrete particular beings and raise the mundane to the marvellous. The reading woman is Barnet's version of the medieval and Renaissance madonnas with one book or two (the bible plus a learned commentary). Barnet's domesticity has one foot in eternity as he speaks for a fresh modernist sense of ancient logos harmony. The supreme light of intellect in the women's faces compares not as much to Leonardo's *Mona Lisa* as to his *Ginevra de' Benci*, a richer and finer study, as well as to the faces of Giotto's madonnas. In these paintings by Barnet, I have ignored the finely wrought abstract formalism, the integration of parts and whole which Longinus also singled out as an elevation to the sublime. While I do not address the issue, for both Taaffe and Barnet, grandeur of scale is crucial and adds its special imprint to sublime subjects.

All of my suggestions about Taaffe and Barnet should be taken as exploratory possibilities hoping for probability. We always seem to need fuller and elusive knowledge when treating living painters. In the case of these two artists (and others), when a clear interest in the sublime is manifest, then the whole accumulated vocabulary of the sublime should be brought into play in the task of exegesis.

Notes

1 This Newman essay is most easily available in *Barnett Newman: Selected Writings and Interviews*, ed. John P O'Neill, int. Richard Schiff, notes Mollie McNickle, Alfred A Knopf, New York, 1990. Newman's comments are on p173.

2 Philip Taaffe, 'Now and Forever, Amen', *Arts Magazine*, March 1986, pp8-9. Taaffe also reveals that like Newman, he has studied the classical literature of the sublime.

3 *ibid*, p9.

4 These remarks come in an interview of Taaffe by Lilly Wei in a series of interviews entitled 'Talking Abstract', *Art in America* 75, December 1987, p122.

5 *ibid*. It is extremely difficult to define Modernism or postmodernism clearly, but perhaps Taaffe has in mind that the deconstruction rejection of any possible privileged theories or values is so paralysing that no one has a sufficiently strong vision of truth or value to engineer a major disruption. If all theories are equally false, why bother?

6 *ibid*.

7 *ibid*. It sounds somewhat as if Taaffe is approaching the ruthless predetermination of atonal music, in which the twelve tone sequence is fixed ahead of time and is exploited by variations. In explaining one phase in which he played with an appropriation of Op art, Taaffe observes (pp122, 171) that he handled works of Bridget Riley to see if he could 'turn an Op painting into a relentlessly expressive thing'.

8 *ibid*.

9 *ibid*, p171.

10 *ibid*.

11 *ibid*.

12 One of the most interesting directions relating to faculty psychology is pursued in the philosophy journals and has an ancestor in Poe: the idea that intuition and imagination are themselves special forms of reason, and that most strong emotions appear only when there is good reason.

13 Dan Cameron, *NY Art Now:The Saatchi Collection* (In G Politi, 1987), p21.

14 *ibid*, p23.

15 *ibid*, p55.

16 *ibid*, p43.

17 Michael Kohn, 'Philip Taaffe', *Flash Art*, No 124, Oct-Nov 1985, p72.

18 *ibid*, p73.

19 Dan Cameron, 'The Other Philip Taaffe', *Arts Magazine* 60, October 1985, p20.

20 Seth Edenbaum, 'Parody and Privacy', *Arts Magazine* 62, October 1987, p45.

21 G Roger Denson, 'Flight into Egypt: The Islamic Reveries of Philip Taaffe', *Flash Art*, No 154, October 1990, pp129-30.

22 *ibid*, pp132-33.

23 *ibid*, p133.

24 Thomas Weiskel, *The Romantic Sublime*, Johns Hopkins University Press, Baltimore, 1976, p2.

25 *ibid*, p3.

26 *ibid*, p4.

27 *ibid*, p5.

28 *ibid*, p6.

29 *ibid*, p11.

30 *ibid*.

31 *ibid*.

32 *ibid*, p23.

33 *ibid*, p24. Weiskel's stress on physicalism and 'realist' terms relates him to the broad new physicalism movement in philosophy.

34 *ibid*, pp24-26. Weiskel apparently perpetuates the false view that Eliot's *The Waste Land* is a negative document. Actually there are three great positive moments: when the protagonist is struck dumb by the hyacinth girl and sees into the heart of light; when the London fishermen are happy beside a great church; and when there is 'a damp gust bringing rain'.

35 *ibid*, pp26, 27.

36 *ibid*, pp27-30.

37 *ibid*, p31.

38 *ibid*.

39 *ibid*.

40 *ibid*, p32.

41 *ibid*, pp36-40.

42 *ibid*, p43.

43 *ibid*, p44.

44 *ibid*, p48. Weiskel (51-54) mistakenly relegates Wallace Stevens to the fully negative sublime by claiming that Stevens never escapes anxiety, finds nothing higher than the self in a state of doubt, and reaches no points of leverage which are transtemporal. Actually Stevens declares that philosophers may show doubt but artists must show positive spiritual faith, that the memory of Major Man is transtemporal across the whole of European culture, and that the green-given structures of eternal nature are stable and transtemporal. See especially Stevens's ode 'Asides on the Oboe', and his essays 'The Relations Between Poetry and Painting', 'The Noble Rider and the Sound of Words', and 'The Figure of the Youth as Virile Poet'. These are collected in *The Necessary Angel*, Faber and Faber, London, 1942.

45 *ibid*, pp65-67.

46 *ibid*, p76.

47 *ibid*, p77.

48 *ibid*, p83.

49 *ibid*, p92.

50 *ibid*, p94.

51 *ibid*, p105.

52 *ibid*, pp137, 152.

53 These mechanisms cannot be explained until brain research clarifies the way in which the brain rewards the mind for favoured actions by releasing pleasure-producing endorphins and hormones.

54 Louis Wirth Marvik, *Mallarmé and the Sublime*, State University Press of New York, Albany, NY, 1986, pp153, 158.

55 *Longinus on the Sublime*, trans. AO Prickard, Oxford University Press, Oxford, 1926, pp13,14.

56 *ibid*, 28-31.

57 *ibid*, 26-27.

58 *ibid*, p49.

59 *ibid*, p65.

60 *ibid*, p42.

61 *ibid*, p49.

62 Kant's *Critique of Judgement*, trans. JH Bernard, Hafner, New York, 1951, p135.

63 *Edmund Burke*, PF Collier and Son, New York, 1939, pp50-51, 54. This is the Harvard Classics edition.

64 *ibid*, p60.

65 *ibid*, p61.

66 Newman's sculptures reflect a Jewish sense of sacred place, and Newman is locating it in the existential present.

67 *op cit*, Burke, p65.

68 *ibid*, p69.

69 *ibid*, pp67-68.

70 *ibid*, p67.

71 Kant's key passages come in sections 23-28 of *The Critique of Judgement*.

72 The importance of this aspect of Kant's theory of the sublime is noted by Paul Crowther in *The Kantian Sublime: From Morality to Art*, The Clarendon Press, Oxford, 1989, p20.

73 *op cit*, Kant, section 7, paragraph 7.

74 *The Birth of Tradegy*, trans. William A Haussman, Russell and Russell, New York, 1964, section 7.

75 Jean-Francois Lyotard, 'Presenting the Unpresentable: The Sublime', *Artforum* 20, April 1982, p69, and Hans-Georg Gadamar, *The Relevance of the Beautiful and Other Essays*, trans. Nicholas Walker, ed. and int. Robert Bernasconi, Cambridge University Press, Cambridge, 1987, pp33, 45, 47, 168-69.

76 Avis Berman, 'Artist's Dialogue: Will Barnet', *Architectural Digest*, February 1986, p62.

77 *ibid*, p66.

78 Caril Dreyfuss McHugh, 'Will Barnet', *Arts Magazine* 59, December 1984, p15.

79 *op cit*, Berman, pp72, 74.

80 Terry Trucco declares that Barnet handles 'idea and themes found in the literature of the New England Transcendentalists'. See Trucco's 'Will Barnet: A Part of and Apart from his Times', *ARTnews* 81, December 1992, p98.

81 Richard J Boyle, 'Will Barnet – The Survival of an Individualist', *ARTnews* 72, October 1973, p82.

82 For instance see Trucco, p95, and Hedy O'Beil, 'Will Barnet', *Arts Magazine* 55, May 1981, p15.

83 *The Critique of Judgement*, halfway through section 29 and earlier in the same section, in the subsection entitled 'General Remark upon the Exposition of the Aesthetical Reflective Judgement'.

84 Robert Doty, *Will Barnet*, Harry N Abrams, New York, 1984, p18.

85 *ibid*, p72.

86 *ibid*, p116.

87 *ibid*, p125.

88 *ibid*, p128.

89 *ibid*, p137.

Will Barnet, Dawn, *1976-83, oil on canvas*

KANT AND MALEVICH
THE POSSIBILITY OF THE SUBLIME
Mojca Oblak

Kant defines sublimity as the capacity of certain phenomena to evoke an awareness of our supersensible self. Vast or destructive natural phenomena ('mathematically' and 'dynamically' sublime, respectively) overwhelm our ability to comprehend them at the level of ordinary perception and imagination and so evoke a feeling of inhibition and pain. But the failure and inadequacy of our cognitive faculties at the sensible level serves only to stimulate the employment of *rational* comprehension. The phenomenal totality of vast items, and immense destructiveness, can be comprehended as an idea – ie in rational terms at the level of thought. This leads primarily to insights concerning our existence as rational beings. These insights have, at the same time, a fundamentally moral import. They exemplify our rational self-sufficiency and superiority over nature. In the final analysis, it is this rational/moral faculty which is absolutely sublime.

However, what happens when we try to transfer Kant's treatment of the sublime into art? Kant stresses that the sublime must be sought only in the mind of the judging subject and not in the object itself. Nature is a means to the experience, but *only* a means to it – and even then, only in so far as it involves *formlessness* and *excess* of magnitude in terms of size or power. Art is nominally excluded from this, since in the artwork 'a human end determines the form as well as the magnitude'.[1] In the history of artistic practice Kant's conception of the sublime as involving the 'infinite', 'formless', 'unpresentable', 'respect' and so on, is used in all possible senses, usually distorted, or without reference to Kant's own philosophical intention. Indeed, in such 'artistic' uses of the term 'sublime', art can represent almost everything: from the stylistically or morally great, sacred, spiritually exalted and elevated, to everything strange, obscure and frightening, Kant's model is also applied to certain works of art in so far as they are physically vast, colossal, overwhelmingly complex or of terrifying power. The sublime can also arise from a quasi-'dematerialisation' of art in the exploration of notions such as light, technology, concepts. In its reference to the 'infinite', art can recapitulate romantic values and images or try to define its own superior rational nature through mystical evocations of the 'unknown'. Tak-

ing all this even further, 'formlessness' (or the absence of form as a possible index to the unpresentable) is seen as a strategy wherein art can disrupt the clarity and purity of formalism and formal beauty through physical, expressive, or excessive transgressions. The recent example of Lyotard's theory of postmodernity indeed connects the sublime to a new sensibility, aware of the possibility of infinite experimentation and development of art as the deconstruction of the natural. What we notice, in general, in almost all these examples (of course, without trying to diminish the value of certain artworks) is the regression of the term sublime into mere 'quasi' images of the 'sublime'. This 'empirical sublime' (as I shall term it) simply replaces the ordinary empirical interest in art with another more 'elevated, but attenuated' function.

The same problem arises in relation to Kant's term 'respect'. In the course of his discussion Kant explicitly links the experience of sublime to the feeling of respect. For Kant the will is free only to the extent that it is motivated by respect for the moral law. (Free will and the will under moral law are one and the same.) In producing such feeling, consciousness of the moral law produces a pure moral interest and even a sense of sublimity of our own transnatural existence. But to act from duty (ie acting under the recognition of the moral law as supremely authoritative and unconditional) should not be equated with the self-imposed tyranny of the rational over the sensual encountered in the 'empirical sublime'. The moral law directs rather than exerts a kind of attractive force on the psychological state of a subject.

So, when we try to justify the whole domain of inwardness and spiritualisation in art in terms of the sublime, we confront a constant mythologisation, where Kant's specific use of the term is corrupted beyond recognition. Transplanted into art, the Kantian term of the sublime is expanded far beyond its original definition and maybe demands radical translation. It becomes necessary to reconceptualise the term itself as well as its manifestations. Kant himself could probably not connect the sublime to art because in his time he had yet not experienced the liberation and autonomy of art. This, of course, only arose after the rejection of basic mimetical qualities,

Kasimir Malevich, Black Square, *1923-29, oil on canvas*

35

thus simultaneously opening possibilities not only of formal autonomy, but of art assuming its *own* responsibility and maybe its own ethical direction.

If the sublime *is* the superiority and autonomy of spirit in the presence of an excessive empirical world, then the real question which arises is how this confrontation with the idea of rational autonomy can find its authentic manifestation in an artwork. From this point of view, art would be entitled to be called sublime only when it could exemplify through form, its own rational self-sufficiency. This involves the rejection of any subservient role as a bearer of ideas no matter how exalted. In the strictest Kantian terms, in other words, sublimity cannot be expressed in an artwork as a content-evoking 'infinite' presence. The feeling of the sublime cannot be aroused by artistic phenomena in terms of the magnitude or power of their immediacy – no matter how excessive they are. Art works are not sublime when they try to impress, touch, frighten or elevate (especially nowadays, when for deadened sensibilities filled up with images and information, shock remains the last effective element of attraction). Rather, the Kantian sublime is only truly attained when art becomes congruent with the possibility of its own radical self-sufficiency and freedom.

Before I proceed further in relation to art I would like to consider some more ideas in relation to Kant's theory of freedom itself. One of Kant's basic theses – that pure reason can be practical – opens the possibility for action which is not wholly determined by laws of nature and the mechanistic chain of causes and effects. This mode of action (which is not simply 'uncaused') is established on a distinct, non-natural kind of causality – *the causality of reason*. In the case of such actions, reason directly exercises its autonomous causal power, and is simultaneously able to produce effects in the phenomenal world. The independence of reason in this sense involves 'spontaneity'. This means that rather than reflecting a pre-given order of nature, reason projects an order of its own. As Kant puts it, 'Reason does not . . . follow the order of things as they present themselves in appearance, but forms for itself with perfect spontaneity an order of its own'.[2] The idea of spontaneity as pure creation *ex nihilo* is a transcendental idea (ie neither derivable from, nor referable to, anything simply given in direct experience). This idea embodies freedom in its transcendental sense, which as a regulative idea – a conception – can determine the ordinary, ie practical notion of freedom and its essential non-empirical quality. This status as 'idea' carries no implications as to its reality or non-reality. As Henry Allison remarks ' . . . it is not

that the reality of transcendental freedom is denied; it is rather that it is not necessary to establish the reality in order to "serve" practical freedom. All that this requires is the conceivability of transcendental freedom, which makes it possible to use the transcendental idea in a regulative fashion as a "model" for the conception of agency and the imputation of actions to agents'.[3] For Kant all free actions are *caused* by reason; those grounded in moral consideration are also *motivated* by reason. To claim, indeed, that reason is practical (in Kant's sense), means that it not only provides rules for actions, but ones, moreover, which have a motivational quality, bound up with the distinctive feeling of respect. Kant's ground for morality, in other words, is established in a pure mode of willing rather than one derived from empirical sources. Now, will – which is itself a supreme law giver (ie gives law to itself) – is autonomous. It is able to act independently of determination by heteronymous (natural) causes and empirical interest. Through moral grounding in rational autonomy, in other words, we free ourselves from mechanical determination and natural causality and act in accordance with our own idea of laws. Reason employed autonomously in moral willing entails obligation grounded upon personal responsibility in the most universal and absolute terms. Its absolute character as a law given by the rational subject to himself or herself, is what makes it great beyond all comparison. The greatness of natural items or properties can only be measured by comparison with other such items. Such greatness is, therefore, finite and dependent. Our free rational/moral being, in contrast, is what makes us more than nature. It is supersensible and can be measured against nothing but itself. Hence, if it is beyond all comparison great, it alone is worthy of the term sublime. On these terms we should see the feeling of the sublime as that which arises when we encounter or experience freedom as transcending and evincing its authority.

Kant's idea of the 'spontaneity' of reason – as a model of pure beginning – and his linking of responsibility to moral will and feeling, can in relation to art prove more significant than passively applied images of Kant's description of the sublime. Such a conception of freedom applied to art would not just involve art's capacity to effect changes in the world by breaking through social, institutional, and natural limitations; it would also open a radically 'creationistic' perspective emphasising the capacity for self-determination. This conception would link both growing rationality and formal autonomy in art and also its autonomous moral direction. The significance of this would be

Kasimir Malevich, Black Circle, *1923-29, oil on canvas*

37

to understand morality as embedded in the formal means of art itself, rather than in the realm of those metaphysical, moral or spiritual insights conveyed or 'suggested' by art.

On the basis of this approach, I would like to consider a definite angle in Malevich's work and his theoretical ideas. It will see him as an example of art's intrinsic link with morality and freedom and, thereby, as an example of Kant's pure conception of the sublime.

The interpretations of Malevich's work are numerous and divergent. In his theoretical texts Malevich refers to many philosophical and artistic ideas which have to be considered carefully, if only because he uses them in idiosyncratic ways. Especially problematic is his idealist-mystical terminology, which is sometimes seen as pointing towards abstract spiritual symbolism. However, as I will try to show, his central term 'non-objectivity' (which alludes to 'nothing') is not the dubious spiritual entity – opening metaphysical avenues – which it is sometimes taken to be. We must also consider the point that – in common with modernist and avant-garde movements in general – Malevich rejects mimetical or narrative functions in art. Again, his rejection (as embodied in the basic principles of Suprematism) differs radically from other modernist and avant-garde tendencies. The purity and self-sufficiency of artistic form in Suprematism is not a demand for self-referentiality and formal autonomy, based on primary elements of colour, shape, volume and so on. Indeed, Suprematism is not defined as a 'colour' but rather as a 'dynamic' problem. (The problem of colour does occur later, in his pedagogical practice, but only as a reflex or addition to Suprematism.) In Malevich's own words, 'many people think that colour in Suprematism is the main thing, that Suprematism is a colour trend . . . a two-dimensional plane and colour phenomenon, but investigating Suprematism, I find nothing of the kind'.[4]

Malevich's formal development of the squares is not derived from the demand of the literal work of art for an affirmation of the image and the two-dimensionality of the support, neither is it a function of the problem of construction as found in Russian Constructivism's combination of abstract forms and elements. In Constructivism, the artwork is primarily the object, and is addressed in terms of objective formal principles of development. Suprematism, in contrast, denies the establishment of any new, applied artistic reality and value. It is precisely this denial of values in general which makes Suprematism radical, distancing it from the mimetical and the image (the 'icon' in the service of 'utilitarian' meanings). To quote Malevich again,

'everything that strives to increase the creative ideas without returning them to the existing imitation, metamorphosis, composition of the existent, or to aesthetisation, maintains the idea of the exact beginning'.[5]

For Suprematism, the highest and purest creative structure is an artwork which in its form does not possess a single relation to the existent. Malevich understands representation not in the traditional sense of depicting real things, but in the sense of a relation to any norm, value or belief which functions as the imposition of religious, social or institutional ideas upon art. His struggle with the mimetical, indeed, is totally at odds with any conception of art as a reflection of ideas and values. Consider the following, 'but the image is something which has to be overcome, because the image is a horizon which impedes my gaze and consequently there is something in it which retards my progress, it is not transparent, but nor is it solid, obstructing the entrance into a sightless world where "I" and the "wasteland" will exist'.[6]

For Suprematism, the mistake of imitative art (as one amongst many other means of expressing the complexity of the world) lies exactly in the idea of expression as such. Suprematist art rejects expression in general – together with the expression of its own Suprematist *idea* – and thus defines itself as pure action.

Suprematism is an artistic movement which has to prove itself capable of rising above a constant regressive tendency. It does not just try to recover a lost sophistication or seek for greater cognitive power as the legitimate mode of artistic self-criticism. On the contrary, it is aware of the dangers involved in following the new values based on rationality and knowledge. Specifically Malevich notes that, 'Cubism, like all practical humanity also believes in knowledge and in the possibility of scientific analysis and synthesis; it believes in culture which, like a master, will construct a key to everything unknown, to everything hidden in gloom. Suprematism has a sceptical attitude towards this master'.[7]

There is an almost 'natural' corruption of any resistance movement to the normative culture and society. This is why Malevich stresses the 'additional element' – an activating force which (in its ability to change the world through effective disruption of the given order) has to be in Suprematism, constantly exercised and forced to its radical limits; constantly escaping the growth of mimetic fixations. Again, in Malevich's words: 'Try not to repeat yourself either in icon or in a picture or in words. If something in your action reminds you of something you have done in the past, the voice of

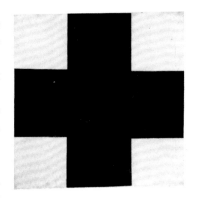

OPPOSITE: Kasimir Malevich, Red Square: Painterly Realism of a Peasant Woman in Two Dimensions, *1915, oil on canvas;* ABOVE: Kasimir Malevich, Black Cross, *1923-29, oil on canvas*

new birth tells me: wipe it off, remain silent, put it out quickly if it is fire, so that the hems of your thoughts will grow lighter and will not get rusty'.[8]

In general, we have to understand Malevich's anti-mimetical impulse as a strategy which dissociates Suprematism from both empirical reality and the functional complex of artistic institution and social norms. Malevich is, however, aware that like every other manifestation in art, Suprematism is just one possibility of understanding. What makes it different and superior is not its radical formal and ideological novelty, but rather its self-consciously expressed demand for freedom: 'Suprematism is also a prism, but the prism through which one does not see a single what'.[9]

For Malevich, then, artistic practice must be radically orientated towards freedom for its own sake. It seeks to transcend the past, and to avoid ossification in the creation of its own institutions and ideas. Following Schopenhauer, Malevich's general conception of the world as 'will and representation' is one which emphasises the constant flow of Becoming. On these terms, phenomena are seen as infinitely transforming themselves from one manifestation into another, ie from 'something' into 'something' as a result of 'blind', competitive forces of rejection and acceptance. In response to this meaningless strife (experienced in an unbearable excessive weight of passivity) Malevich tries to create a system of art which can transcend the crushing nightmare of the blind causal flux through the free 'harmony of weightlessness'. This idea at once discards the fetished and constantly mimetical system of art, and questions the possibilities of art as such. It focuses most clearly in Malevich's central term of 'non-objectivity': 'Everywhere there is a faith and hope, and truly it can be said that happy are those "who believe", since for those who do not believe there remains nothing, ie non-objectivity'.[10] Non-objectivity exemplifies a radical emancipation from the imposed patterns of imaginary and institutional identifications constantly opening an empty space: 'Therefore the struggle for his essence, for existence, is at the same time a struggle for non-essence. And he will also have a non-objective (aimless) view of being.'[11]

From this point of view, Suprematism's rejection of representative and aesthetic tendencies is founded in non-objectivity as *absolute detachment*. At the same time, through opposing the natural current of the world, non-objectivity becomes a principle of activity as the basis of volition. Malevich relates this to the position of the Suprematist artist as follows: 'He says that the blind elements surrounding him, physical conditions of nature, influence his consciousness; he wants to rid himself of these

influences via his consciousness; he wishes not so much to overcome them completely but to regulate his relationship'.[12]

Suprematist radical demand for free act of volition finds its proper and final manifestation in the course of the development and understanding of artistic form itself. The artwork and its meanings are directed solely by a moral drive towards freedom and autonomy. Only on this basis can art reject every semantic and symbolic relation with reality and (in the idea of form determined by free beginning, also every mimetic character: 'I am free only when my will – established on the critically philosophical basis – is able to carry out the foundations of the new phenomena'.[13]

In contrast to dependent mimetical art (defined as 'slavery before causality'), Suprematism must prove itself through becoming its own cause (ie 'free from all causes'). This means that it must strive to build its own forms on the basis of pure abstract 'aimless' necessity – 'outside time and space' and, thence, on its own causality. ' . . . the form only begins when the link of elements begins, in the main guided by the artistic beginning . . . As, in the final reckoning, elements do not exist in "the world" . . . they arise from our own intention'.[14]

Suprematist art, therefore, involves spontaneous beginnings where the world 'disappears' and 're-appears' again – free from arbitrary or mechanically determined factors. Suprematist art creates its forms *ex nihilo* as a new system of necessities, relations and appearances. Freed even from the most basic elemental determinations, Suprematist forms progress through their own logical space, dividing into lines, planes, colours, volumes and combining again in constructions and systems.

The purest example of the spontaneous beginning as the primary manifestation of form is probably Malevich's description of his *Black Square* itself. 'The square framed with white was the first form of non-objective sensation, the white field is not a field framing the black square, but only the sensation of the desert, of non-existence, in which the square form appears as the first non-objective element of sensation'.[15]

The later development of the system of squares and its formal consequences – signifying temporal transformation – manifests itself directly without trying to express anything further. Non-objective 'colourless' energy gradually annihilates in white, ie in a complete absence of all representations and associations. (Such associations, indeed, only survive to a limited degree in black.) The system of squares establishes itself in rationally formal self sufficiency. Malevich's idea of artistic forms rearticulated in a new order of elemental relationship, opens up a massively new conception of art. For all its obscurity, eccentricity or incoherence, Malevich's demand for freedom in art is (in my judgement at least) the most radical and sustained attempt to deal with this problem in the entire history of Western art. And if sublimity in the Kantian sense, in its final consequences, involves a feeling of our possessing a pure and self-sufficient reason, imposing its dominion over sensibility, then Malevich's art is entitled to be regarded on the same principles. In Malevich's case, this link with the sublime is even stronger than in those works usually tied to the concept (ie ones involving quasi-philosophical images of infinity, formlessness, power and so on). Malevich makes art instantiate and declare those capacities for reason and freedom which sustain artistic form in its purest sense, and so, through the idea of spontaneous beginning and formal causality alone, establishes the grounds of art's own moral direction. It is a pure rational self-sufficiency.

Such an artistic position (which does not ask the question 'what is the picture', but rather, 'is art outside any idea and ideology – does it differ from everything?') cannot avoid entering constant and radical insecurity. The collapse of all traditional formal foundations in art tends towards forms which are unfamiliar in their defiance of every pre-established universality. Creating 'without an idea', as creating *ex nihilo*, differs from everything in institutionalised reality. Malevich's 'unseen' nature is an aspect which is unrecognisable precisely because it is caught in conflict between ordinary imagination and reason. That is why Malevich's apparently clear and self-evident forms oppose every imaginary and rational simplicity. Their hermetic character is not founded on irrationality or formal self-referentiality but as the inhibition of ordinary, imposed recognition of images and associations. This inhibition is the basis of a radically non-mimetic rational function and can, as I have shown, be related to the idea of the sublime. This is because it involves both negativity and an ultimate affirmation of the power of reason in art.

Maybe Malevich's model is especially useful today, when art confronts its own absolute uncertainty. His approach is opposed to that mirroring of present disintegration in art which involves an empathic and empirical sublime identification with the forces which threaten to overwhelm us. This 'sublime' is simply a repetition of old strategies. It involves, as it were, a familiar image of what is supposedly unfamiliar and threatening. Malevich, in contrast, avoids the pictorial rhetoric and 'elevating' content of the empirical sublime. He returns us, rather, to the sublime, in its authentic Kantian mode – as an affirmation of the dignity of freedom and reason through art.

Such a conception of the sublime – based on a transition from the excess of greatness and power to the possibility of free action – is possibly more of a force for coherence than the present trend towards shock and disintegration. At the same time, however, its uncompromising non-mimetic stand does not allow the comfort of old securities. We might say that it manifests absolute sublime *uncertainty*, ie uncertainty without those consoling images and the rhetoric of uncertainty, which characterise the empirical sublime.

Notes

1 Immanuel Kant, *The Critique of Judgement*, trans. JC Meredith, The Clarendon Press, Oxford, p26.

2 Immanuel Kant, *The Critique of Pure Reason*, trans. NK Smith, The Macmillan Press, London and Basingstoke, 1973, A548, B576.

3 Henry E Allison, *Kant's Transcendental Idealism: An Interpretation and Defense*, Yale University Press, New Haven and London, 1983, p328.

4 Malevich, *The World as Non-Objectivity (Unpublished Writings 1922-25)*, Vol III, trans. Xenia Glowacki-Prus, Edmund T Little, ed. Troels Andersen, Borgen Copenhagen, 1976, p82.

5 Malevich, *The Artist, Infinity, Suprematism (Unpub-lished Writings 1913-33)*, Vol IV, trans. Xenia Hoffman, ed. Troels Andersen, Borgen Copenhagen, 1978, p49.

6 *op cit*, Malevich, *The World*. . . p288.

7 *ibid*, p88.

8 *op cit*, Malevich, *The Artist*. . . p13.

9 *op cit*, Malevich, *The World*. . . p91.

10 *ibid*, p10.

11 *ibid*, p225.

12 *ibid*, p152.

13 *op cit*, Malevich, *The Artist*. . . p144.

14 *op cit*, Malevich, *The World*. . . p56.

15 *op cit*, Malevich, *The Artist*. . . p146.

SUBLIMITY AS PROCESS
HEGEL, NEWMAN AND SHAVE
Richard Hooker

I

Particular to definitions of the crisis of culture associated with Modernism has been the idea of a self-conscious and inward-looking approach to the production of representation. Artists and philosophers alike are held to have become newly aware of problematic assumptions which sustained, but compromised, earlier less self-conscious systems of representation. Under Modernism, philosophers examined the way their arguments were conditioned by language and reason, and painters became preoccupied with surface and the texture of paint, absorbing themselves in the conditions of painting. Within this general definition of Modernism, the relation between art and philosophy had been revealed to be unstable and often contradictory. For example, Greenberg famously identifies Kant as the first modern philosopher, due to his inward-looking examination of the rational basis of philosophy. A related tendency in painting, however, according to Greenberg, did not emerge until the late 19th century. More confusing still, Greenberg's own argument, *qua* representation of the development of modern painting, has been criticised for being too dogmatic and inflexible. Despite identifying a modern crisis of representation in philosophy and painting, his own critical position suffers no such qualms. Taking Greenberg's argument as a totality in this way, reading it as both a representation of Modern painting and as an analysis of representation *in* painting, the contradicting ways in which his argument engages with the idea of Modernism is revealed. The apparent inconsistency makes it difficult to identify the Modern 'crisis' as either all-consuming or historically defined. On evidence of the way Greenberg frames his argument, the idea of a blanket 'Modern crisis' seems an oversimplification: philosophy, art and criticism respond to and define this crisis in different ways, at different times.

One reason for the apparent inconsistency is that Greenberg's deployment of the general definition of Modernism is mediated by the particular material circumstances of its manifestation. Where philosophy becomes self-conscious of reason, the crisis of painting is likewise contained by the specific material limitations of its medium. Greenberg argues that with the decline of the aristocracy and the invention of photography during the 19th century, painting lost its traditional audience and had its representational function usurped by photography. In response, painting, like philosophy, developed a characteristically inward-looking Modernist tendency, but did so as a reaction to the material pressures which directly affected it. That Greenberg's criticism does not respond to the crisis he diagnoses elsewhere is because, as criticism, it is immune to the effects of the material pressures which have a specific impact on painting.

Against this kind of piecemeal dissection of different categories of representation, more global attacks on representation *per se* have emerged. To take an obvious example, Marx dismantles ostensibly 'natural' and 'universal' ideas and behaviours, revealing them to be underwritten by hitherto transparent and overlooked interests. His critique derives its strength from its seeming ability to transcend traditional Humanist divisions between art, philosophy and criticism, revealing interests that underpin the bourgeois culture. At the same time, Marx also reverses his deconstructive momentum, replacing old systems of representation with his own accounts of what underwrites it. His argument therefore aims to destabilise particular assumptions about the neutrality of representation, ultimately affirming its legitimacy through his own partial diagnosis of what 'really' enables representation to function.

Partly as a theoretical response to this contradiction within Marxism, a second, harder threat to stable meaning emerged in poststructuralism. Here a kind of circularity is generated where representation is perpetually defined and redefined as radically unstable and ultimately deficient in its attempts to represent the world. As such, these arguments are interesting because they suggest themselves as a potentially revealing philosophical parallel to developments in recent art. Like Marxism, however, poststructuralism has gained a reputation for its seeming capacity to transcend traditional disciplinary boundaries with its claims to undermine representation as a whole. By comparison with the modernist approach which Greenberg represents, the destructiveness of poststructuralism

FROM ABOVE: Terry Shave, Stalker 4, 1992-93, oil paint and nylon flock on canvas; Terry Shave, Reflections I, *1993, oil paint and nylon flock on canvas*

at all levels presents a difficult problem for philosophically informed attempts to use it to illuminate like tendencies in recent art. On the one hand, against Greenberg's ostensibly inviolate critical position, artists, philosophers and critics are represented as being in the same boat; no one can claim to be outside the unstable condition of meaning poststructuralism suggests. On the other hand, if poststructuralism reveals meaning as unstable and deficient, then, to be consistent with itself, this condition of meaning must be taken to apply to all the traditionally secure relations that are held to pertain between philosophy, art and criticism. We cannot take for granted the critical distance Greenberg assumes. So, if Greenberg's theory provides a sophisticated, but flawed, example of how philosophy, art and criticism might be seen to relate, his strategies cannot simply be uplifted and transferred to this different philosophical, artistic and critical environment. Not only is Greenberg's critical argument too rigid, unable to respond to the particular dualities of individual paintings, but the self-conscious tendencies of Modern philosophy on which it is based have been transformed and extended by poststructuralism. Equally important, art has changed and developed beyond the conditions Greenberg saw as defining it. Under these conditions, especially given the sceptical implications of poststructuralist argument, the whole relationship between art, criticism and philosophy needs to be understood as radically unstable.

If there is a lesson to be learned from Greenberg and a critical disposition demanded by poststructuralism, then it is that criticism itself must become conscious of the way it constitutes itself in relation to its objects. That this is rarely, if ever, the case is obvious, even in the work of self-declared poststructuralists. It is as an author that Barthes is famous for having proclaimed the 'death of the author'. In the foreword to *The Post-Modern Condition*, Fredric Jameson points out that Lyotard's book is a narrative which diagnoses a crisis in narrative.[1] These arguments overtly question and undermine representation, but simply because we can understand them, they affirm it. This contradiction is not necessarily wrong in itself because it can be mobilised in a productive way. Some poststructuralist texts make a gesture towards internal consistency by attempting to deconstruct themselves, but as often happens, this contradiction becomes transparent and only imaginarily resolved. Given this potential for confusion in the pursuit of what could be interesting convergences between poststructuralism, criticism and art, we need to be clear about these two different categories of poststructuralist argument. One undermines what it diagnoses as inconsistencies in other examples of representation, but in so doing, seeks to reveal itself – examples of representation – as inevitably engaging in similar inconsistencies. The other simply re-inscribes the inadequacies diagnosed in the object of its criticism by failing adequately to declare and reveal its own.

A way to draw out the various implications of this important distinction and the grounds on which it might be seen to extend to painting, is to consider that poststructuralism as a whole, despite its inconsistent quality, has generally been defined – and has defined itself – against European Humanism. It has become something of a cliché to say that in contrast to poststructuralism, the Humanist tradition represents a broad faith in the rational project and thus assumes the adequacy of representation. This common understanding of the incompatibility between these apparently antithetical cultures is revealed in a very different light by an argument of Hegel's which distinguishes between different categories of scepticism.[2] This is important because it provides a way of thinking about poststructuralism in terms other than as a simple contradiction of Humanism.

Hegel identifies Pyrrho as an exemplary sceptic, who, believing in the absolute fallibility of all representation, literally withheld his judgement by writing no books. Out of Pyrrho's absolute scepticism a different stage emerged when his strategy was developed by others, becoming a philosophical school which defended its own views and argued its own case. In so doing, however, according to Hegel, such scepticism became internally contradictory. Although its beliefs had not changed, the simple process of *articulation*, of engaging with language and representation, affirms their persistence and inevitability, no matter what lengths are gone into disowning them. Now, as we have seen, when poststructuralist arguments are defined as simply anti-Humanist, they seem completely destructive of representation, but in the terms of Hegel's argument, this is shown to be an oversimplification because such arguments implicitly affirm representation to convey their sceptical message. Instead of poststructuralism, *qua* anti-Humanism, placing meaning in jeopardy, meaning is revealed by Hegel as something which is impossible to avoid if we do not, like Pyrrho, remain silent. If Hegel's terms of reference undermine the image of poststructuralism as anti-Humanist and absolutely sceptical, how might the same criteria apply to Modern painting which is sometimes presented as the negation of all previous art?

II

In Greenberg's terms, Modernism in painting is described as the progressive revelation of its material qualities. The emphasis on material here derives its contrast with illusion and traditional illusionistic painting wherein material qualities are consciously played down, so as not to contradict a painting's likeness to something outside itself. What is important about this argument is not only that the material quality of paintings should be given positive emphasis, but that it should be emphasised as the negation of illusion. Against this negative definition of a painting's material quality, Hegel's argument, when it is extended to painting, suggests a different way of characterising the material quality of Modern painting. In terms of Hegel's argument, this material is neither simply anti-illusion, nor does it replace illusion with some other formal or expressive system, but has meaning simply through its having been *presented*. Obviously Expressionist and Formalist arguments emphasise different ways in which the material quality of nonillusionistic paintings have meaning. Both, however, ultimately rely on ideas of order – either internal structure, or relating to the emotions – to suggest that the material of paintings points beyond itself. From the perspective of Hegel's argument, the material quality of painting has a meaning by simply being manufactured, staged, presented: any of these words which, in painting, suggest the difference between the silence of Pyrrho and the utterances of those who articulated and defended his position. A painting, regardless of its illusionistic, formal or expressive quality, is different from its surroundings because it has been set apart for particular attention.

This notion is most clearly emphasised when we consider Minimal art which seems to remove all traditional 'art' qualities *except* its having been presented. Frank Stella, although not usually considered a Minimalist, produced his 'Black Paintings' which sought to highlight their 'made' quality to the exclusion of all else. From a Humanist perspective these works are empty and cynical but considered in another way, as differentiating themselves from silence and suspension of judgement, their quality is as a simple 'thisness', a having been presented. It was once put to Stella in an interview that his work seemed to pursue an 'economy of means' – a quality they certainly possess when compared with most other art. He replied: 'Yes, but there's something awful about that "economy of means". I don't know why, but I resent it immediately. I don't go out of my way to be economical. It's hard to explain what exactly it is I'm motivated by, but I don't think people are motivated by reduction. It would be nice if they were, but I'm motivated by the desire to make something, and I go about it in the way that seems best'.[3]

Stella's response reveals that he did not identify the motivation for his work solely as a response to other art, by comparison with which it was certainly reductive, but in *the desire to make something*. In terms of its production, and at its most basic, art is the simple manipulation of materials. It is very easy for critics and historians who look at and judge art in terms of its relation to other art, and in writing about it – an activity which does not involve much manual manipulation of material – to overlook the significance of this mundane, but nevertheless defining aspect of art's character.

Just as Minimal art distinguishes itself from its environment as simple material, so can parts of paintings distinguish themselves from more traditionally meaningful passages within the same work. A mark with an illusionistic, anti-illusionistic, expressive or formal function, might, against these qualities, simply declare its 'material', distinguishing itself from its surrounds. 'Material' here is meant in the very widest sense and is not specifically a term to designate a quality particular to 'art'. It might simply describe a contrast, for example the distinction between a painting and the wall on which it is hung. It might describe the difference between a snail's trail and the surrounding ground, or a piece of litter on a road, or a mark on a piece of paper. 'Material' in this sense is a contingent quality which rests in the distinction between presence and absence.

From a critical perspective this idea of the simple 'material' aspect of art presents a peculiar conundrum. Criticism places its emphasis on explaining why works of art are different from each other and different from other objects. Expressionist and Formalist theories imply that every mark or gesture in a work of art can be explained as meaningful in terms of it having some expressive or formal *content*. The idea of 'material' delineated above implies a less stable quality contingent on a contrast between ideas of presence and absence of meaning which are themselves fluid. It hence follows that criticism which engages with the idea of 'materiality' in art, cannot aspire to the degree of authority claimed by Formalist and Expressionist critics. To do so, to inscribe 'material' with a definitive meaning or content, would be to negate it. Perhaps the obvious response to this dilemma for criticism would be to follow Pyrrho's example and say nothing! This, however, would be to avoid the problem. Furthermore, the very instability of the idea of a painting's 'material' quality demands a level of critical commitment that more easily ac-

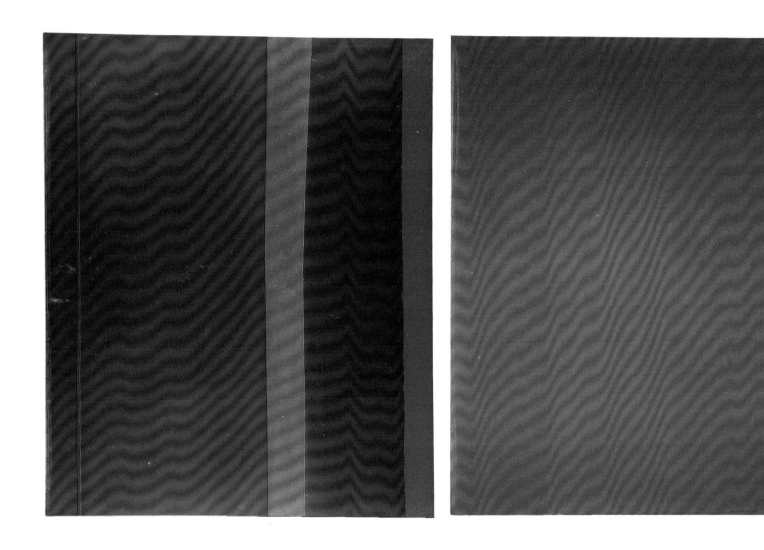

cepted characteristics do not so obviously demand. A more positive way to confront the dilemma is through the philosophical category of the sublime which, especially in Kant's and Hegel's explorations of the theme, can be read as focusing on precisely the problem of representing those phenomena which by definition cannot be represented.

III

A problem facing attempts to describe art in terms of the sublime has been the fact that Kant's analysis, which, while certainly the most suggestive, limits the sublime to the experience of nature. Accordingly, the most obvious but least interesting extension of the sublime into art has been to declare that art attains a sublime character through representing nature as overwhelmingly powerful. Caspar David Friedrich's paintings are conspicuous examples of this kind of art, but all they can ever do is represent situations in nature where we might experience the sublime if we were there. They are paintings which could make a claim to represent situations which might evoke a feeling of the sublime, but they cannot evoke in us the experience of the sublime.

Much more suggestive and interesting is the argument that there is a parallel between poststructuralist arguments and some recent art in their common capacity to evoke the experience of the sublime.[4] The basis for this claim has been to relate the dynamic of Kant's argument to poststructuralism and some postmodern painting. Broadly speaking, Kant's account of the sublime involves two movements. The first is the experience of an object which overwhelms our conceptual and imaginative capacities to the extent that we cannot conceive of, or represent, its totality. The second is our acknowledgement of this incapacity. The second movement transforms the negativity of the first because our ability to acknowledge and represent the object which overwhelms us *as transcending us*, serves to emphasise our cognitive powers. By way of conveying how poststructuralist arguments might be characterised as engaging the terms of Kant's definition of the sublime, it has been argued that the two movements of his description are embodied in poststructuralism's revelation of all representation as insufficient. Poststructuralist positions identify representation as always insufficient, but the very fact that they give expression to this insufficiency affords such positions the capacity to evoke the experience of the sublime. In a parallel argument, the idea of the sublime has been applied to painting which disrupt straightforward assimilation by simultaneously suggesting contradictory readings.[5]

While this argument provides a very interesting framework for a discussion of the relation between poststructuralism and postmodern painting, by identifying the sublime with postmodern painting *per se*, it does somewhat preclude the possibility of deploying the idea in more specifically defined circumstances. Part of the problem here is that the notion of the breakdown of representation and the associated idea of the world as 'unpresentable', have become such familiar motifs of postmodernism that they are easily alluded to without being engaged. Postmodern painting is riddled with devices signifying representation as problematic: Schnabel's broken crockery stuck to the surface of his canvases diffuses the images painted on it; Baselitz's upside-down paintings short-circuit unselfconscious attempts to read them; Salle's layers of images present unreadability as their definitive condition. Precisely because these devices so plausibly relate to the tenets of poststructuralism, the relation between painting and criticism risks assuming a Greenbergian rigidity quite at odds with the claims of either poststructuralism or the ostensibly disruptive aspirations of these artists.

A way around such shortcomings in art and criticism might be to identify art which engages with the idea of sublimity more rigorously than the above examples, and to apply the theory itself in a way that is more critically engaged. The most tangible obstacle to these aspirations, however, lies neither in the art nor the critical strategy, but in Kant's own argument which locates the experience of the sublime in the mind, rather than in any particular object. Obviously a theory that uses Kant to explain art in terms of its putative sublimity must resolve this problem, but in a way that remains true to the dynamic of Kant's position. Hegel's development of Kant's theory is a particularly suggestive example of how this might be attempted. Like subsequent interpretations of Kant's theory of the sublime, a central problem for Hegel is to extend its interesting implications beyond its restriction to the experience of nature. Hegel is particularly keen to preserve the ambiguity implicit in this aspect of Kant's theory, and to this end he seems to read 'nature' as signifying not only the opposite of reason or human artefact, but as a conscious refusal on Kant's part to come to a more determined definition of material stimuli for the experience of the sublime. Hegel is not being original here; he is simply placing emphasis on what he sees as an essential aspect of Kant's argument, an excerpt of which he quotes: 'For the sublime in the strict sense of the word, cannot be contained in any sensuous form, but rather concerns ideas of reason, which, although no ad-

LEFT TO RIGHT: Barnett Newman, Adam, 1978, oil on canvas, and Eve, 1988, oil on canvas

equate presentation of them is possible, may be excited and called into mind by that very inadequacy which does not admit of sensuous presentation'.[6] This sentence seems ambiguous as to what precisely is presented to consciousness in an experience of the sublime. First, Kant is clear, the sublime 'cannot be contained in any sensuous form'; second, 'it concerns ideas of reason', but neither can these be adequately presented. Third, what can be represented is the inadequacy we experience in trying, but failing, in the first two moments just described.

The important theme Hegel amplifies is the idea that the object which precipitates the sublime experience must remain inadequately presented to consciousness in order that inadequacy can be represented. As soon as the experience of the sublime is linked with a specific object, that object is defined either sensuously or rationally, which precludes it from evoking our experience of the inadequacy of these faculties. It might seem logical to argue that since not all phenomena evoke in us the experience of the sublime, we can designate certain of them as being sublime in themselves. If we do so, however, even in the most rudimentary way, using words like 'ocean', 'mountain', 'the night sky', we have represented them to consciousness. No matter how insufficient these words are as representations of what they signify, *unless they are consciously held to be insufficient*, they have already precluded that feeling of inadequacy which defines the sublime. This thesis looks circular and pedantic, but it is the focus of Hegel's development of Kant's theory which places special emphasis on holding the different 'moments' of Kant's argument together: 'The sublime in general is the attempt to express the infinite, without finding in the sphere of phenomena an object which proves adequate for this representation. Precisely because the infinite is set apart from the entire complex of objectivity as explicitly as an invisible meaning devoid of the shape and is made inner, it remains, in accordance with its infinity, unutterable and sublime above an expression through the finite'.[7]

There are two essential parts of this description. First, for Hegel, the sublime involves an 'attempt to express', involving an action, a striving. Second, this 'attempt to express' confronts 'something' which is 'explicitly an invisible meaning devoid of shape'. These two moments of Kant's theory, as Hegel reads them, are held together as definitively incompatible. It is this incompatibility which is sublime: 'This outward shaping which is itself annihilated in turn by what it reveals, so that the revelation of the content is at the same time a

supersession of the revelation, is the sublime'.[8] Here Hegel emphasises the sublime as the *process of representing something which cannot be represented*, whereas Kant locates the experience of the sublime as a mental response to the failure of this process. As a consequence, for Hegel, sublimity is no longer necessarily identified as taking place only in the mind, where it is realised.[9] For Hegel, therefore, sublimity as process can be extended to a different, but parallel context, namely the process of painting or drawing where the same kind of unresolvable tension between representation and unrepresentable object might be thematised.

If this framework is now applied to, say, Schnabel's crockery paintings, or Baselitz's upside-down paintings, then these disruptions of the image are precisely that – 'disruptions' – but there is no way they are radically incompatible with the process of representation. On the contrary, in the atmosphere of postmodernism one might even say the opposite. These are gestures which acknowledge contemporary ideas of representation as definitively problematic, but which, once made, enable the artists to continue representing in what is actually a traditionally unproblematic way. Both Schnabel's broken crockery and Baselitz's inverted images serve as gestures towards the idea of the disruption from the process of representation itself. Like Barthes and Lyotard, they explicitly disown or destabilise representation, but they only represent that disruption, they do not engage with it.

IV

To suggest criteria for art that might more plausibly relate to the Hegelian principle of sublimity, it is necessary to recall the idea of a work of art as 'material'. This quality I suggested can give a mark a definition outside its function as illusionistic, anti-illusionistic, formal or expressive. Just by *being*, it resists categorisation as meaningless. For a painting to reveal this quality, however, it cannot simply be 'invoked' by a critical reading. It must emerge out of the process of manipulating material in the attempt to represent an unpresentable subject. It is where representation reveals itself as problematic in this process that we might expect to identify sublimity in painting. Under these conditions there exists the potential for an artist to mobilise the tension between a mark or gesture as aspiring to content by representing its subject, but in the very process of attempting this impossible task, the mark simultaneously declares itself as 'material'. To reiterate, using Hegel's words again, the sublime is where 'the revelation of content is at the same time a superseding of the revelation'. The terms for applying Hegel's argument to painting can be clarified with the analysis of some of Barnett Newman's work. Newman's painting is often associated with the idea of the sublime, in part because of his own interest in the idea as demonstrated in the titles of some of his paintings and in his theoretical writing about the process of painting.[10] While this is interesting in itself, it does not tell us if any of his paintings are sublime according to Hegel's criteria. That some of Newman's work does fulfil these criteria can be arrived at by juxtaposing two very different accounts of his work. Robert Rosenblum has discussed Newman's *Onement, I* in the following terms: 'Newman's *Onement, I* of 1948, the first in a series by this title, already transmits, in supremely small dimensions, the effect of sublimity that Newman would explore and aggrandize until the end of his life. The stark bisection of a coloured field with a vibrant vertical shaft of glowing, fiery light suggests again the domain of primal creation, and it has even been proposed that the imagery alluded to in the title is related to Kabbalistic texts describing the first creation of man. At the very least, [it] is as drastic an image and structure as Friedrich's vision of the beginning of the universe'.[11]

Rosenblum here presents an argument which identifies the sublimity of Newman's work as deriving from the fact that it 'transmits' or 'alludes to' sublime events: 'Primal creation', 'the first creation of man', 'the beginning of the universe'. He even likens Newman's work to the archetypal representer of the sublime, Friedrich. As I have already proposed, this kind of analysis of a painting's sublimity relies on the notion that it absorbs that quality from its object. This does not define Newman's work as sublime according to Hegel's definition of sublimity. Keeping Rosenblum's judgement in mind, however, consider Donald Judd's following description of another of Newman's paintings: '*Vir Heroicus Sublimis* was done in 1950 and the colour of one stripe was changed in 1951. It's eight feet high and eighteen long. Except for five stripes it's a red near cadmium red medium. From the left, a few feet in, there is an inch stripe of a red close in colour but different in tone; a few feet further there is an inch of white; across the widest area there is an inch-and-a-half of dark, slightly maroon-brown that looks black in the red; a few feet further there is a stripe like the first one on the left; a foot or so before the right edge there is a dark yellow, almost raw sienna stripe, the colour that was changed. These stripes are described in sequence but of course are seen once, and with areas'.[12]

Donald Judd here simply describes the material qualities of one of Newman's paintings. Now, obviously, Rosenblum and Judd have different axes to grind. Rosenblum wants to locate Newman within the framework of his construction of a 'Northern Romantic tradition'. Donald Judd, one of the most important Minimalists, by contrast writes about Newman's work in such a way as to show why he found Newman's work interesting, and to link it with his own production. Despite the clearly partial perspectives from which these writers are working they do, I believe, represent equally legitimate and common responses to Newman's work. At times, one of his paintings may evoke in us the idea of 'primal creation' or any one of the sublime scenarios Rosenblum identifies as their content, but, at the same time we are aware of what we are looking at as coloured rectangles divided by vertical lines. Rosenblum's way of describing Newman's painting is not wrong in its allusion to the elevated content of the work, but it does not acknowledge another contradictory but equally strong characteristic, highlighted by Judd, which is as simple 'material'. In Judd's description, Newman's painting *Vir Heroicus Sublimis* is represented in a way that is not significantly different from, say, the experience of looking at the side of a truck. For the position Rosenblum represents, Judd's way of looking at Newman probably seems a cynical travesty of the esoteric pseudo-religious and 'spiritual' aspirations Rosenblum identifies in Newman's work. This, however, is to define the 'material' quality Judd finds so important as the simple negation of Rosenblum's way of seeing. It is not. In the context of attempting subject matter which is unpresentable, the inability to present it cannot be a failure; rather, it is the refusal to remain silent in the face of a hopeless task. This quality does not reside 'in' Newman's painting, but as 'material' in its contrast with the blank wall on which it is hung. It is in the incompatibility of Rosenblum and Judd's ways of seeing and representing Newman's painting that I propose the latter's work is revealed as sublime in the Hegelian sense. Newman is such a significant artist in terms of the idea of the sublimity of painting because his work explores the tension between the hubris of attempting to represent something which cannot be represented, and simply declaring itself as 'material'.

From a critical perspective, the challenge presented by the juxtaposition of Rosenblum and Judd's readings of Newman's paintings is to encompass their very different ways of seeing without attempting to resolve them. Of course, any mark in any painting can be critically defined as 'material', especially if we use poststructuralism as a method of critical intervention. Equally, and more often, critics define all art and all aspects of art as meaningful by resorting to Expressionist or Formalist theories. Against both kinds of theoretical overdetermination – one which is predisposed to citing the absence of meaning, the other its presence – criticism needs to be flexible to avoid the predetermination of its objects and to be able to respond to the particular qualities of individual works, or groups of work, that engage similar problematic elements. This is an especially important requirement when painting is the object of criticism. The failure of language to represent the world adequately, in the manner delineated by poststructuralism, is a relatively consistent feature. That is to say, the difference between sign and signified is not presented by poststructuralism as being qualitively different between, say, the word 'cube' and a real cube, or the word 'sphere' and a real sphere. When these two items are drawn or painted, however, it is easier to produce a representation of a cube than a sphere. In other words, there are degrees of success and failure to represent in painting that owe at least something to the qualities of the subject matter. This is not meant to signal a hard and nonexistent distinction between the conventionality of language and the immediacy of visual images. Rather, a difference which seems particularly pertinent at the level of production to the difference between the distance implied by *describing*, and the immediacy of *making*. Extrapolated to the idea of 'material', the same argument holds. The way a painting declares its material can be significantly different according to the context of its manipulation. Is 'material' suppressed with the attempt to produce an illusion? Is it revealed with the conscious aim of undermining traditional representational systems, or the conscious desire to produce a painterly parallel to poststructuralism in painting? Or, is it revealed through the process of attempting to present something that cannot be represented? A meaningful critical response to the idea of the 'material' quality of painting certainly needs to be informed by a broad theoretical strategy, but it also needs to be able to respond to these particular contexts through which 'material' is revealed.

Terry Shave is a contemporary artist whose work thematises its 'material' quality through a variety of these strategies and any attempt to define his work in terms of its relation to the idea of sublimity in painting must be correspondingly flexible. Like Newman's, Shave's paintings and prints seem to be animated by an unresolvable tension between their simple material quality and the attempt to represent an unpresentable subject. Unlike Newman's paintings which declare their 'material', 'non-art' quality principally through their colour and blankness, Shave's present themselves as 'material' through a wide variety of mark-making techniques, relying on contrast between them, rather than on a single dominant texture or colour. Accordingly, the parameters for defining sublimity in his work shifts from the overall contrast between seeing the content of a whole painting and seeing its 'material'. With Shave's work it is more a case of identifying the process of sublimity in the contradictory functions of a particular mark, or between different parts of a painting, or even in the contrast between individual works.

Flexibility in confronting Shave's oeuvre at these different magnifications, so to speak, is necessary because his work does not generally have Newman's finality. This is not necessarily a failing on Shave's part. As with most Abstract Expressionism, Newman's work testifies to a confidence in the ultimate significance of painting which, in retrospect, seems more in the gift of the particular artistic, critical and political atmosphere of post war New York, than the aspirations of any single individual. This is not to say the shifting tendencies Shave's work embraces are all equally successful. If they were, there would be no need to change, but the revisions and transformations of his work since the mid 80s suggest a restlessness and dissatisfaction that cannot be reduced to the idea that he has not yet achieved a 'stylistic maturity'. This may be a result of a more honest symptom of the attempt to deal with the sublime tension between 'material' and unrepresentable content than Newman's paradoxical authority.

Given the historically changing dynamic of his production, it is logical that Shave has chosen to organise and present his work as a succession of series. Each has a title that seems to relate loosely to its content and typically includes paintings and prints linked by common motifs, evolving strategies for the manipulation of painterly and printed material. The title of the *Fall to Pandemonium Series*, 1990, suggests it might deal with some epic mythological event; an impression reinforced by simple representational devices in the etching; a low horizon, perhaps the ocean, and an emblematic 'V' shaped 'bird' in the top centre, which is almost solid black, its representational function potentially reinforced by the rest of the print which, given its lighter tone and the presence of the 'bird', might read as sky. Between the 'bird' and the horizon is a vertical trace of lighter tones which could be read as a suggestion of movement. At the same time, the status of this mark within the loosely defined narrative framework is more ambiguous than the other elements. It is a representational mark. What it represents is not some recognisable aspect of the narrative, but the material of the plate from which the print was taken. In making prints from this series, the artist not only used the traditional etching processes which corrode and remove the metal of the plate, he added various materials to its surface, most notably car body filler. This is not an elegant material, nor is its presentation elegant; sections of the print seem to declare themselves as errors, inadequately repaired and erased by the filler which leaves its own imprint. In other parts, sharply defined marks look like attempts to cross out what lies beneath them. The heightened crudity contradicts and almost literally obliterates the epic narrative content.

From a wider perspective, the friction this print embodies between epic content and its presentation is echoed in Rauschenberg's *Erased de Kooning Drawing*. According to one of the stories which grew up around this event, de Kooning's drawing was done with grease pencil, ink and heavy crayon. As a result it took a month and forty erasers for Rauschenberg to satisfactorily erase the image.[13] What makes it so potent are the physical lengths to which Rauschenberg went to destroy de Kooning's drawing, while preserving its 'material' existence. Quite unlike Newman's work, whose 'material' quality is revealed as the absence of any obvious making, de Kooning's, as the epitome of 'gestural' Abstract Expressionism, achieves its impact through the skilful touch of the artist's hand. Rauschenberg's erasing is a symbolic negation of this tradition, but it is just as handmade and equally tactile. The artist does not skilfully apply pigment, holding the eraser he works the surface, removing one kind of mark and replacing it with another.

Shave's work in general and this *Fall to Pandemonium* etching, in particular, pulls together and incorporates some of the disparate themes suggested by Rauschenberg's gesture, especially its physical nature. Whereas the impact of Rauschenberg's erasing is contingent on our understanding of de Kooning's reputation as the most technically accomplished draughtsman of the Abstract Expressionists, Shave's work internalises the differences between Rauschenberg and de Kooning, and, more importantly, it is made concrete in the context of the attempt to present a subject matter which is only imagined and incompletely resolved. The sublimity of Shave's etching resides in the way its final state both records and represents the schizophrenic conflict between artists working in the tradition of fine art etching, representing unpresentable subject matter, and the worker, unable to satisfactorily represent, messily obliterating the artist's traces.

Shave's paintings from the period share similar preoccupations, but without the suggestion of barely controlled nervous confusion that this print develops so successfully, and which seems to resonate forcibly with Hegel's definition of sublimity as process. A painting from the *Estuary Series*, as the title suggests, is identifiable as a traditional landscape, unlike the *Fall to Pandemonium* etching. The content is more readily available to the viewer and relatively easily resolved, effectively evoking and representing an idea of the magnitude of nature. Countering this content and the illusion of space it creates, the upper left half of the painting is interrupted by various gestural marks that declare themselves as surface, but also the hand of the artist. Obviously this painting engages with the same kind of problematic pursued in the *Fall to Pandemonium* etching, but because the activities of the hand erasing and creating are demarcated in this painting, there is a more detached exploration of sublimity than in the etching. It is as though we are looking at the landscape through a dirty window that disrupts, but does not completely confuse our vision, we can hold the two apart in a way that is quite impossible in the *Fall to Pandemonium* etching.

In 1992 Shave's painting changed in ways that significantly shifts the framework within which their potential sublimity might be seen to operate. *Walkabout 1*, for example, might have been similar to the painting from the *Estuary Series*, but half of it has been obliterated with a sheet of black nylon flock, stuck to its surface. The black flock conceals the paint beneath it, cutting it off with a simplicity that is almost violent. The calculating nature of this gesture is emphasised by the fact that the edge of the black flock cuts the painting exactly in half. Here the operation of negation and concealment of representational marks has become the negation and concealment of paint, but it is not just that, the black half of the image has its own definition as a single mark, as 'material' presence. Precisely because the painted right half has been obliterated, the subject matter of the painted left has become uncomfortably ambiguous. The impossibility of seeing the rest of the painting, which might provide clues to its narrative content, gives it a tenuous and unstable quality curiously related to the dynamic confusion of the *Fall to Pandemonium* etching, short-circuiting easy assimilation in a different way. Like the painting from the *Estuary Series*, different painterly behaviours are clearly demarcated, but in *Walkabout 1*, the difference cannot be easily accounted for and absorbed. Rather, they animate the process of looking by making it problematic in a way that more obviously fits with Hegel's definition of sublimity as process.

Some of these themes have been developed in more recent work where the artist has continued to exploit the difference between areas of oil painting that create an imagined space, and areas of flock that conceal and contrast with it. For example, *Stalker 4*, 1992-93, is dominated by a central area of oil paint that penetrates an imagined space which, while related to the earlier, more overt allusions to landscape, is less easily definable as such. The feeling of space is contradicted internally where the material of the paint appears as stains and dribbles. The way the flock is used, its colour, shape and position, make it blend into the oil painted area, except as the thin black vertical line on the right edge. As in *Walkabout 1*, the flatness of the flock and the texture of the oil paint serve to emphasise their respective material qualities, but the difference is not as stark because the different ways of manipulating material become more subtly juxtaposed. It as though the vertical strips of flock fragments form the visual equivalent of inverted commas around the central painted illusory space.

The four examples of Shave's work discussed here illustrate something of the range of his integrated and diverse explorations of subject matter associated with traditional painterly attempts to deal with the idea of the sublime. Using Hegel's argument as a critical basis, however, it can be argued that Shave's work extends this tradition far beyond the limitations of Friedrich's work, and beyond the cul de sac of Newman's and Rothko's paintings. His ability to do this resides most clearly in his extended conception of the idea of representation as the process of manipulating material – a theme he explores in surprising and revealing ways which simultaneously engage and expose new ways of defining the instability of representation, whether in the status of an individual mark, the organisation of his whole oeuvre, or somewhere between them.

Notes

1 Jean-Francois Lyotard, *The Postmodern Condition: A Report on Knowledge*, trans. G Bennington and B Massumi, Manchester University Press, 1984.

2 GWF Hegel, 'Relationship of Scepticism to Philosophy: Exposition of its Different Nodifications and Comparison of the Latest Form with the Ancient One' in *Between Kant and Hegel*, eds. George di Giovanni and HS Harris, SUNY Press, Albany, 1985. For a useful discussion of Hegel's argument see Robert R Williams, 'Hegel and Scepticism', *The Owl of Minerva*, Vol 24, No 1, Fall 1992, pp71-83.

3 Bruce Glaser, 'Questions to Stella and Judd', *ARTnews*, September 1966. Reprinted in *Minimal Art*, ed. Gregory Battcock, Dutton and Co, New York, 1968, p159.

4 Paul Crowther, 'Beyond Art and Philosophy: Deconstruction and the Post-Modern Sublime', *Art & Design*, March 1988, pp46-52.

5 *op cit*, Crowther, pp50-52.

6 GWF Hegel, *Aesthetics*, trans. TM Knox, The Clarendon Press, Oxford, 1975, Vol I, p363.

7 *op cit*, GWF Hegel, *Aesthetics*, p363.

8 *ibid*, p 363.

9 *ibid*. Hegel writes: 'This [the sublime], therefore, differing from Kant, we need not place in the pure subjectivity of the mind and its Ideas of Reason; on the contrary, we must grasp it as grounded in the one absolute substance *qua the content which is to be represented*. The classification of the art-form of the sublime is likewise derived from the above-indicated double relationship of substance as meaning, to the phenomenal world', p363.

10 See, for example, the paper by Barnett Newman, 'The Sublime is Now', *Tiger's Eye*, Vol 1, No 6, December 1948, pp51-3. Reprinted in *Art in Theory: 1900-1990*, eds. Harrison and Woods, Blackwell, Oxford 1992, pp572-74.

11 Robert Rosenblum, *Modern Painting and the Northern Romantic Tradition: Fiedrich to Rothko*, Thames and Hudson, London, 1975, p210.

12 Donald Judd, 'Barnett Newman', *Studio International*, February 1970. Reprinted in *Modern Art and Modernism: A Critical Anthology*, eds. Frascina and Harrison, Harper & Row, London 1982.

13 Daniel Wheeler, *Art since Mid-Century: 1945 to the Present*, Thames and Hudson, London, 1991, p129.

Terry Shave, Walkabout I, *1992, oil paint and nylon flock on canvas*

DAMIEN HIRST AND THE SENSIBILITY OF SHOCK

Loura Wixley Brooks

'The Jack the Ripper of the Art World', 'Media Darling', 'Public Enemy Number One', 'the dirty geezer who sells the dirty trainers and underpants for 10,000 quid' *(Art Monthly,* June 1994, p8). All this and more has been said about Bristol-born artist Damien Hirst. Not since André has an artist stirred up so much controversy, disgust and publicity. Hirst is on the crest of a wave, the forerunner of a new tack British contemporary art has taken, with the rest of the world hastening to follow suit. Is he in it for the money? Undoubtedly he is. Unpredictable and innovative he may be, but he is not stupid. By creating works with an intense edge and disgusting, unsettling subject matter, Hirst has invited everyone back into the arena for discussion of art's role in contemporary life, along with what actually constitutes art. His recent installation, the purpose of which is to generate publicity for Daniel Moynihan's opera *Agongo* was one of the most talked about works at the 1994 Edinburgh Festival. The headlines tended to focus on the living constituents of the piece – rats – rather than the more interesting confrontational aspects of Hirst's works. As an example of this taste for confrontation, he recently said in *Art Monthly,* 'if you go up to anyone in the street [and show them some of his work] they would just say "What a pile of fucking total bollocks, it's shit, I've never seen anything like it", and to me that's just what it is. Art has to be able to stand up to everything else and if it can't then it doesn't work . . . if you have an idea of an audience then it has to communicate with everybody . . . '[1]

Does an art like this need any sort of legitimising discourse? Not strictly speaking, but perhaps if it can be shown that all this disgusting presentation is part of an on-going, well established creative tradition, and that there is a strong and clear philosophy of the sublime to support this sort of work, then perhaps appreciation can take the place of outrage. Hirst's works can be terrifying to behold; they are capable of producing strong nausea and deep fear. It is through this evocation that we try and understand how best to approach Britain's most publicised, if in some circles, least popular, artist. I shall approach Hirst's work by first considering a possible meta-theoretical matrix for it in Edmund Burke's theory of the sublime.

I

First published in 1757, Burke's *Philosophical Enquiry into the Ideas of the Sublime and the Beautiful* was extensively revised before republication in 1759. It introduces some basic concepts which are still of use to us today. As his starting point, Burke draws a distinction between what he terms as 'positive pain' and 'positive pleasure'. He uses the term 'positive' simply because he deems both these human responses to be active on the state of mind of the subject as opposed to non-active, or latent. Pain and pleasure are not, however, dependent on each other for their effects, one can feel pain without noticing an absence of pleasure, and vice versa. If one is in a normal state, which he terms as 'indifference' or 'tranquillity' and one then has a pleasurable experience, one would not say that previous to that experience one was in any state of pain, nor does the removal of the pleasurable factor entail any pain.

Taking this a step further, Burke argues that there is a difference between the removal of pain and any positive pleasure: 'for when we have suffered from any violent emotion, the mind naturally continues in something like the same condition, after the cause which first produced it has ceased to operate'.[2] Once this terror or pain has subsided, we are moved back to a state of indifference, perhaps tinged with a memory of our recent horror, but certainly not in a state of positive pleasure. The term Burke uses for this state of being is 'delight', a relative sort of pleasure. It is 'the sensation which accompanies the removal of pain or danger', not necessarily sublime, but closely akin to it.[3]

Burke further contends that there are two ideas most capable of making an impression on the mind, and that these are self-preservation and society. Of the latter, he seems to regard love and its loss as the most likely to cause strong emotions, and likens a jilted lover's grief to a positive pleasure. The idea of a human being's instinctive self-preservation as it is acted upon by terror, however, has more bearing on our later discussion of Damien Hirst's work and its aesthetic effects. Self-preservation is one of the strongest human emotions, and anything which resonates on that instinct can be

Damien Hirst, In and Out of Love, *1991, gloss household paint on canvas, butterflies, MDF boxes, table and ashtrays with cigarette ends*

one of the keys to a sublime experience. Burke's whole theory of the sublime hinges on this very thing; even if dangerous things are mediated by their physical distance from us – or as in the case of art, the picture plane itself – self-preservation and the emotional and visceral resonances that instinct provokes when we gaze on terrible objects or depictions is the instigator of sublime feeling.

Burke explains this as follows: 'If the pain and terror are so modified as not to be actually noxious; if the pain is not carried to violence, and the terror is not conversant about the present destruction of the person, as these emotions clear the parts, whether fine, or gross, of a dangerous or trouble-some encumbrance, they are capable of produc-ing delight; not pleasure, but a sort of delightful horror, a sort of tranquillity tinged with terror; which as it belongs to self-preservation is one of the strongest of all the passions. Its object is the sublime'.[4] The highest degree of this is astonish-ment, with respect, awe and reverence close be-hind. These states of mind are not possible to connect with any possible pleasure, and therefore must come under the notion of delight outlined earlier. It is in this capacity that things which are not actually dangerous can produce a sensation akin to pain or terror, but of positive significance.

Burke's theory, like many others of his time, overreaches itself, and tries to explain almost everything it encounters. It is possible, however, to tease out some useful threads that have relevance to postmodern art. The differences between posi-tive pain and positive pleasure are of use, as is the statement that we are generally in a state of tranquillity or indifference, in that they provide us with a comparative framework in which to place our sensations of the sublime. Beauty can connect us to the sublime, but as Burke laboriously explains, it is much easier and more straightforward for terror to do this as it reacts on the strongest of human emotions: self-preservation and fear of death.

Any enervating shock is also capable of being a delight to us; imagine a roller coaster ride. We get off the machine refreshed and full of adrenaline. We know intellectually that we have not been in any serious physical danger, but emotionally, and more importantly, physically, we do not. The body's reaction to being hurtled about produces in our minds what Burke terms 'delight tinged with terror'. His explanation about human perceptual faculties can still serve us with a few modifications for our use in postmodern culture. We need to examine some of our culture's overriding characteristics in order to see if we can place some of Burke's points into this puzzle.

II

'Generation X'. 'The Baby Busters'. These terms and others have been applied to both my and Damien Hirst's generation. Postmodern life has a nihilistic flavour; we are besieged by advertise-ments, life is full-on, right in your face, up close and personal, and undeniably fast. The quality of human experience has changed greatly since Burke's time. He lived and wrote at the threshold of the Industrial Revolution, whereas we are now reaping its results in a gloomy, post-industrial world that can seem apocalyptic at worst, incomprehensible at best. Theories of hyper-reality abound, and we are swept along helplessly by the 'information highway' towards an unknowable conclusion. The leading lights of postmodern theory all seem to have a nihilistic edge, an overriding notion that life on this planet is moving far too quickly for any sort of ideology to catch up with us and stabilise our ride. Baudrillard writes of a 'procession of simulacra', wherein the distinction between reality and the representation of reality is erased. Without leaving our homes, or indeed our television sets, we can almost know what it is like to ski, swim with sharks, parachute, or walk through the Prado. It is specu-lated that in the future, virtual reality will be widely used as a teaching tool as well as a means for safe sex. This causes all sorts of moral concerns about virtual rape, computer pornography and countless other angst-ridden, yet unimagined bogeymen. The plugged-in quality of life in this century is inescapable, and it would be idiocy to assume that this has had no effect an our general behaviour. Multi-billion dollar industries have sprung up, geared towards what we can do in this newly created leisure age. An almost infinite menu of ersatz experiences is presented to us for use as a diver-sion from our actual lives, which we seem to spend being indoctrinated by an ad-man's concept of what is normal, and once this is understood, we conform with all speed and effort.

Postmodern life, with all its manically intrusive, infinite variety of administered experience and ideologies, ironically becomes a tedious continuum of monotony, where choosing how to divert oneself from one's actual life is in danger of becoming a greater task than actually living it. This enforced lassitude of course deadens our sense of being alive. The fact that humans are capable of not using their physical and mental faculties and the subsequent atrophy of the mind and body is on what Burke based his physiological explanation of the sublime. In the postmodern era, this indolence is no longer willed, but practically forced on us by the mental overload brought about by the furious pace and variety of administered experiences.

If, as Burke argues, our sense of the sublime is rooted in our instinct for self-preservation and our innate fear of death, then our sensation of being alive is transmuted into a felt quality by witnessing things which feed into these emotions. In any video shop anywhere in the world, we can find acres of blood-and-guts action movies, a wide variety of garish and explicit facsimiles of bloodshed. In America, a series called *Faces of Death*, with actual footage of dead and dying people is presented as entertainment for those whose palates are jaded by fictitious representations of violence, or even the raw actuality that is ever present on the evening news. Paul Crowther has interpreted the need for such 'entertainments' as an 'existential sublime'; a deliberate engaging of life-negating imagery to a life-affirming effect. This need for negation forms the basis of a multi-trillion dollar industry, and, in terms of art, can be employed as a contemplative exercise, on the parts of both viewer and artist.

The aesthetic need for this is what gives rise to 'shock' art, which can be defined as any art in which the primary goal is to appeal to what Burke terms as the most basic of all our instincts. This can occur either through an actual physical reaction on the part of the viewer, or the provocation of mental anguish, confusion or terror, which is transmuted into physical sensation by our physiology. Shocking as it is, it is not intrinsically morally reprehensible, but Crowther gives a few instances in which it can be. The first is if the violence is caused for the enjoyment of others. No one can say that the *Faces of Death* series is all that savoury, but no one was killed for the purposes of the films, so it cannot be dismissed as entirely amoral. The lack of consideration for the families of the victims is reprehensible, but the compiler of this series did not himself do any violent acts. The second way in which enjoyment in witnessing violence or pain can be morally corrupt is if the enjoyment impedes assistance to the victim. We hear stories of rescue crews being impeded in their efforts by bystanders gawking at the pain and death of a traffic accident. The third way in which the depiction of – or the act of actual – violence is morally wrong is if the enjoyment of the suffering contributes to that suffering – as in a torturer leering over his victim and compounding the inflicted physical pain with mental anguish. In spite of having to traverse this moral ground as a matter of conscience, witnessing violence is not a moral wrong in itself since it is extrinsic to the viewer.

In art we are given a further step to take away from the actual suffering itself by virtue of art's very nature as a representational thing. It is in this sense that Burke's 'safety clause' comes into play. The physical distance from an awe-inspiring avalanche that protects us physically without interfering with our sublime experience, in terms of art, is given to us by the picture plane, the fact of representation, or our ability to psychologically distance ourselves at will from that which we see represented. Whether or not we become immune to our physical and mental reaction to depictions of, or actual, violence by virtue of monotonous repetition or abundance of such imagery is most likely a matter of degree of personal experience. However, the fact remains that we all must come to grips with our mortality in some fashion. As Crowther puts it, 'in order to cope with the complex problems of finite embodied existence, it is necessary at some point to look . . . negation of life squarely in the face'.[5] This, I would now like to argue, is exactly what Damien Hirst and others like him do for us, the spectator. Because life-negating imagery or any image which has death as its referent resonates in our selves on or near the self-preservation instinct, it can not be qualified as anything other than a sublime experience.

III

When asked by Adrian Dannat in an interview for *Flash Art* in 1993 if entropy was a central theme to his works, Damien Hirst replied he did not think there was a basic theme to his work, but that he was interested in entropy in a way: 'the contradiction is that you worry about your complexion but you'll be a skull in less than 100 years'.[6] It is this sort of ironic commentary that enables us to see humour, relevant social comment and life-affirming aspects in Hirst's work, once we have overcome our initial gut reactions to some elements he presents us with.

Hirst seems to have made a glorious entrance to his career; the debate about his work leaked out of the realm of art criticism into other media early on. He has provoked aesthetic discussion from the most unlikely quarters, and the publicity surrounding his work has propelled him to a leading position in British contemporary art. Is he a mere sensationalist, however? He deems it necessary to be provocative because 'you have to get through to somebody'.[7] This he certainly appears to have done, perhaps even more vociferously than André's pile of bricks in the Tate or Turner's paint pot could ever do. Because his media are so varied and unusual for what certain of the more philistine British art press are accustomed to, a decided amount of sensationalism will follow. The catalogue for his most recent curatorial effort, *Some Went Mad . . . Some Ran Away . . .* includes such diverse media as blood, wax, dead sheep, urine, metals, plastics, formaldehyde, and the ever present glass tanks. Without the obviously iconoclastic impact of *Piss Christ*, Hirst still manages to infuriate many people, and intrigue many others. We need to look at his career in some detail, as well as his more important pieces and shows before we can decide whether he has any legitimate aesthetic statements to make.

Publicity seems to be a necessary evil for the financial success of any artist these days, and we must not discount Charles Saatchi's role in the start of Hirst's career. Hirst's pickled shark, properly titled *The Physical Impossibility of Death in the Mind of Someone Living* – the phrase itself seeming to echo Burke's sentiments – was purchased by Saatchi in 1991 for £87,000.00. This figure is reportedly close to what the work cost to make. Hence, there does not seem to be too outrageous a profit motive on Hirst's part here, though it certainly is a figure only very few of us would be able to consider paying for a work of art. The debate about Saatchi as either a serious collector, or merely an over-financed sort of art playboy does not concern us here, but the fact that he was lampooned in an independent cartoon along with some of Hirst's work (in which John Major is shown in the pickling solution) is an indication of just how provocative some of Hirst's work can be.

Another work from the Saatchi collection was also lampooned. 'Troy Noggis's Frozen Bogey Nose' is a thinly veiled allusion to Marc Quinn's *Self*, a cast of the artist's head, filled with his own blood and then frozen. It appears in the cartoon with 'Dead Pigeon in Attic Water Tank' along with Charles Saatchi, who buys the two for a one with a lot of zeros beside it. Like Hirst, Quinn says 'I try to make pieces that deal with the basic questions with which one is confronted just by being alive'.[8] Indeed, Quinn's work is provocative. We have a physical reaction to seeing the work, but this gut reaction on contemplation, soon gives over to a sublime one. Doing a self-portrait in one's own blood is actually admirably thorough; not only are the physical dimensions of Quinn's face represented, but his blood type and genetic fingerprint are also permanently present within it: we in the postmodern era are involuntarily and abundantly aware of such scientific concerns and developments. Short of cutting off his own head, Quinn has made as much of a self-portrait as is possible.

Hirst has made a similar proposition. To him the ultimate violent and divisive art act would be to microsurgically remove his own hand, display it, and then hopefully re-graft it back onto his-arm. What are we to make of an artist who would consider self-mutilation a viable artistic proposition? Of course things like that are going to make the papers, but journalists and artists alike have a vested interest in sensational ideas. I would interpret Hirst's proposal as an indication of how seriously he considers his own themes. Hirst's works nearly always involve some sort of death or entropy, or they evoke the uncertainty we instinctively connect to these ideas, which in itself is sensationalist. As stated earlier, looking death in the face is a life-affirming act, and according to Burke's (among others) sensibilities, a sublime experience. Hirst seems to have gone to an extreme in his own gathering of experience: the publicity photograph for one of his first solo exhibitions shows the artist smiling beatifically, cheek to cheek with a severed head in a morgue. Photographs of violent death figure largely in Hirst's work, a photograph taken for *Creative Camera Magazine* is captioned 'Self-inflicted injuries. The deceased has removed his genitals, cut his throat through a full circle and punctured both eyeballs, all with blunt scissors. Though the police suspected murder, the picture is typical of self-mutilation associated with mental disorder, in this case paranoid and religious delusions'.[9] Hirst sees beauty in the freshly dead corpse, still slumped in the place where it was found. In Burkian terms, our first reaction to this is physical and then mental, once we read the caption and then understand the cause of these horrific wounds. The fact that anyone, however mentally unhinged, would do this to themselves is extremely disturbing to our sense of mortality, self-preservation, and even sanity. Being forced to acknowledge the raw brutality of an act in which most of us would consider such an action unthinkable, affirms our own sense of being alive, even if it is alive in the sense of feeling our innards work harder by virtue of being nauseated.

We need to focus now on a few of Hirst's major installations and environments. The most exemplary of Hirst's oeuvre is *In and Out of Love* which took place in a disused shop in Woodstock Street in 1991. There was less overtly visceral imagery on display in this instance: on the top floor, the viewer was greeted by a puff of warm, moist air, the purpose of which was to create the ideal growing and hatching environment for a rare species of Malaysian butterfly. The pupae were placed on stark white canvases underneath which were placed tropical plants and bowls of honey from which they could draw nourishment. The exploded chrysalises, along with the blood that was a by-product of the butterflies' birth were left behind on the canvases to form a collage of shrouds, a reminder of leaving a past state of being behind. The butter-

flies were free to fly around and above the spectator, who found himself placed in a self-contained ecosystem in which he was a privileged observer. This has been referred to as the 'In Love' part of the proceedings. The 'Out of Love' part was installed downstairs, where the solid white canvasses were replaced by garish housepaint colours, on which the butterflies were sloppily adhered, the paint sometimes obscuring the delicate pattern and beauty of their wings. Where the bowls of honey had been, there were now overflowing ashtrays. Birth, rebirth, life and death surrounded the viewer in an inescapable manner.

A similar work by Hirst was entitled *One Thousand Years*, in which a rotting horse's head was the birthplace and food for fly maggots, who, like the butterflies, were free to fly about the room, unless they flew into an insect-o-cutor device – in which case the viewer was privy to their execution. Both these works make great reference to the transient quality of life and the finality of death in an inescapable way, the insect-o-cutor serving as a wry reference to the sometimes randomly vicious behaviour of the universe. Another work, *Pharmacy*, 1992, also makes use of the insect-o-cutor; this time the device is placed in front of an almost overwhelming display of pills, powders and panaceas. The message is overwhelmingly clear; in spite of our best, most sleekly packaged and up to the nanosecond efforts, death is irresistibly inevitable. Hirst remarks about it that 'we should all take that on board as a positive thing. If you admit you're going to die, it makes you more able to live, I hope'.[10] This statement ties in very neatly with Burke's ideas – by being terrified, or even mortified at the notions of death Damien Hirst presents us with, we are again affirming our life by the terror of witnessing death, either by physical revulsion (as the smell of the decaying horse's head in *One Thousand Years* must have provoked) or the mental anguish caused by seeing the beautiful butterflies in one room carelessly plastered on a joltingly coloured canvas in the next in *In and Out of Love*.

These works are by far some of the least overtly offensive of Hirst's oeuvre, but they do serve to exemplify the aesthetic that Hirst is trying to achieve. If it does not provoke in us the sensation of the sublime exactly as Burke describes it, it comes very close indeed to that sort of sublime experience. The upper room of *In and Out of Love* appeals to the sublime on the grounds of the delight we take in being surrounded by delicate winged creatures of exceptional natural beauty, and the lower room is resonant of the sublime in the Burkian sense of terror. We are not threatened with death ourselves, but we are surrounded and mercilessly confronted by it, and our instinctive feelings are acted upon whether we like it or not.

Conclusion

It now remains to place Damien Hirst and his contemporaries into context. A recent exhibition at London's Serpentine Gallery, curated by Hirst, gives us much food for thought as to how British, and indeed much other contemporary art may be related to Burke's theory of the sublime. The title is taken from an essay by Angus Fairhurst, one of the show's contributing artists and in full it reads, 'some went mad, some ran away, the great majority remained faithful unto physical death; modern mystics without God'. Hirst, impressed by this when he read it in 1989, decided that it would be a good title for an exhibition. It is a powerful statement, evoking both postmodern tension as well as an extremely emotionally-charged event. Given the inevitability of physical death, it seems the ones who remained faithful had little choice in the matter apart from desertion or madness; the unspecified mysticism is necessary to carry them forward, since they are without a God to whom they can appeal. It is to this unspecified mystical power that the show makes much of its reference. There is an overarching sense of chaos as an essential element to the fabric of the universe. A seemingly random aggregation of images and themes clash and swarm around us, serving both as a reminder and an exemplification of that innate chaos.

This was not Hirst's first experience of curatorial work: whilst still a student at Goldsmith's in 1988, he organised *Freeze* which launched his career and several others in a blaze of publicity due to public outrage and consternation. Another show, *Modern Medicine*, 1990, was not as easy to create, according to Hirst himself. He likens *Some Went Mad . . . Some Ran Away . . .* to *Freeze*, in the sense that the show seemed to put itself together, whereas *Modern Medicine* required more effort. There did seem to be a strong thematic coherence to this collection, although the works within it were of disparate styles, media and execution. Setting Damien Hirst's own contribution of two works aside (a lamb in formaldehyde entitled *Away from the Flock*, and a quasi-minimalist dot painting), we can try to determine the nature of this thematic unity, and once determined, whether our understanding of it can be expanded by consideration of Burke's existential variety of the sublime.

There are only five British artists represented at the exhibition at the Serpentine Gallery: Damien Hirst, Marcus Harvey, Abigail Lane, Angus Fairhurst and Jane Simpson. There is no particular use in discussing whether there is any coherence to their

Marc Quinn, Self, 1991, blood, stainless steel, perspex and refrigeration equipment

work; nationality does not have very much bearing on this move toward chaos in contemporary art, except that if any artists can be credited with getting the ball rolling, they are by and large British. What I wish to do now is examine four works from artists of various nationalities to determine if what has recently occurred in British art has had any global echoes.

The first of these is Ashley Bickerton's *Solomon Island Shark*, 1993. Hanging by its tail as if caught in some environmentalist's worst nightmare, a hammerhead shark made of black PVC, rubber and leather is the one of the first works the spectator encounters. The shark becomes a fetishised object, the sadomasochistic overtones provoking an involuntary sexual frisson which is amplified by the fact that it is suspended helpless as if in sexual offering to us. A yellow liquid, a reference to urine, is contained in the sacs which hang down its sides, along with coconuts. Not as directly threatening as Hirst's piscine work, it nevertheless is evocative of the struggle between life and death. Perhaps sympathy is evoked by its entanglement in the coconuts, sacs, and what looks like a whip – perhaps not. Regardless, it is a confrontational object; the form is threateningly muscular and its materials associate it unmistakably with a subcultural sexual deviation which embraces pain, helplessness and humiliation as some of its central elements.

The next work, Andreas Slominski's *Untitled*, 1987-88, is composed of a high jump and crash mat, set behind a glass panel in a room with an open door which is also made of glass. It was not part of the exhibition proper, but it features in the catalogue. On closer inspection of the photograph of the piece, we realise that in order to actually do a high jump, we would need to hurtle ourselves through the pane of glass, landing on the mat behind it, inevitably lacerated. Again, the sublime impact of this work is transmitted through the idea of pain and danger. An innocuous piece of physical education equipment becomes for us, the viewer, a potentially life-threatening object. If it were actually used, instead of a graceful arc over the bar to a safe, soft landing, this piece would cause severe, painful injuries or even excruciating death to its user. Like most of the works in the show, its impact is essentially bound up with its unsettling qualities.

Moving away from sculpture for a moment, let us consider Hiroshigi Sugimoto's photographic contributions. Both are silver gelatine prints of waxworks. It is not immediately apparent that they are, in fact, pictures of wax dummies, so the initial effect of seeing the *Bride in the Bathtub Murder*, 1994, is that of seeing a real event. The subject is grisly. A Victorian gentleman peers over the body of his victim as if to be doubly sure that she is dead, while nonchalantly drying his hands. The naked body of the young woman sprawls in the tub, her head clearly underwater, eyes and mouth open, seemingly still horrified at what has happened to her. The sublime effect of this is very much as Burke describes; mental horror followed by a physical reaction as the full impact resounds on our instincts. The smug look on the killer's face compounds the feeling of helplessness as we gaze in sympathy on the innocent looking body of the victim. In this work, the cruelty of human life and indeed the universe is reflected. For all that it is a wax simulation of a real event, a tableau constructed for our visceral entertainment and shock value, in the split second while we are still unsure of its veracity, we experience an existential instance of sublimity.

The next work, a painting by Alexis Rockman, entitled *The Concrete Jungle IV*, 1992, echoes one of Hirst's own statements regarding his overall vision of the show. He intended that the show should be 'like a Breughel or a Bosch painting, or some sort of combination of the two . . . I just see it as chaotic'.[11] Rockman's attention to detail and jewel-like colours certainly do echo Breughel, and the subject is evocative of Bosch at his most turgid. In a semi-submerged scene, we see a wide cross-section of everyday human effluvia: Coke cans, used tampons, plastic drinks strapping and shit floating in diseased-looking green water, along with a dead seagull and a struggling rat. Puffs of sewage emanate from an outlet, and all manner of carrion and waste-feeding fish flow over the surface of the canvas. This is clearly an environmental statement, and is also uncompromising in its ordinariness: this patch of water could be anywhere, in any country in the world. An unpleasant slice of life is presented to us in an almost photographically matter of fact manner, and as it dawns just what is floating on and under the surface of the water, our reaction is at once both mental and physical; moral outrage at the rotting bird trapped in rings of plastic, and physical revulsion at the tampon and the shit. There is also some of the delightful variety of the existential sublime here – the close attention to detail and the smooth finish make this a technically satisfying painting, once the initial shock of the subject matter and its presentation fades.

The final work to examine is *Misfit*, 1994, by British artist Abigail Lane. A waxwork portrait of Angus Fairhurst, another artist in the show, this work is the most socially disturbing of all. Slumped pathetically on the floor, eyes downcast, the semi-nude figure looks forlorn and alienated. The title

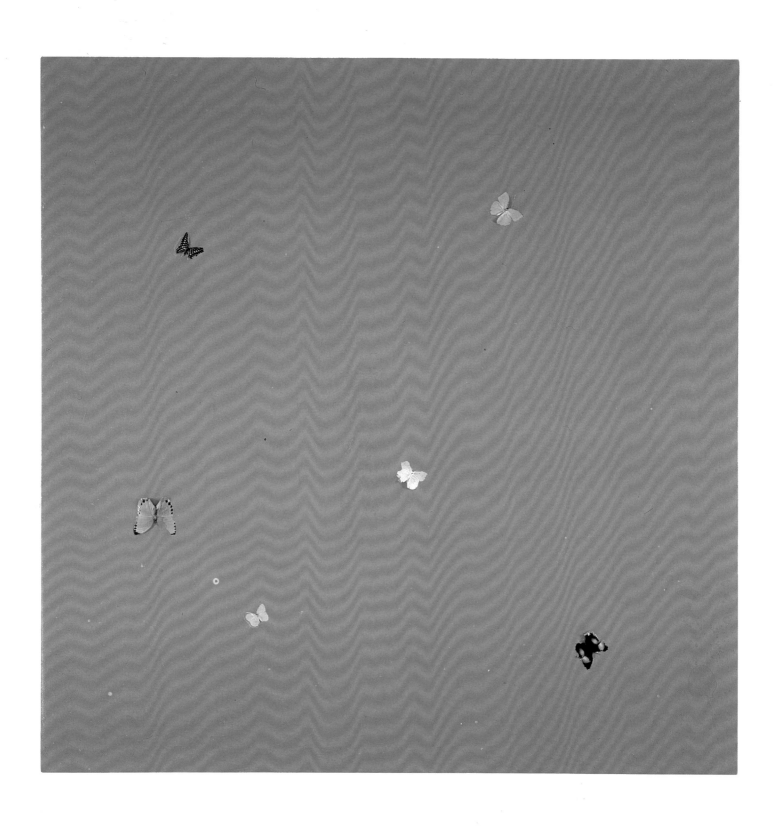

leaves us no room for manoeuvre here. This is a social outcast, whose unabashed lack of trousers completely upset polite social convention, while at the same time his obvious dejection strikes a chord of guilt. 'Misfit' as a title indicates that this person has no place in the world, but his pathetic posture unashamedly evokes our sympathy; his seeming avoidance of our gaze causes us to re-evaluate our own so-called dignity. This figure is beyond feeling the trousers-down anxiety many of us have, and to be lower than that is low indeed. In this work there is a strong sense of alienation: we would probably be inclined to have as little as possible to do with this person if we encountered them in real life, and when forced to look upon him in the art gallery context, we are compelled to consider our own place in the world. While this does not strictly rank as a terrifying experience (I find it rather more tragic than frightening), the importance many of us place on social position and the way this work plays upon that angst conjures a question, 'will I look like that if it all gets taken away?'

The fears of loss and alienation are very powerful emotions in postmodern society, and by causing these fears to rise in us, Lane makes use of the existential sublime very effectively. What is common to all these works and others I have not covered here is the sense of helplessness and alienation that pervades them all. The shark is trapped, the bride in the tub was powerless against her attacker, the misfit seems beyond help, and the glass beside the high jump is unavoidable. Only Rockman's painting suggests a potential for change, but the decay it represents is almost overwhelming: the dead seagull is beyond aid, and like the bride or the shark, resounds with finality. There is a strong chaotic element to the exhibition. As a whole it has been likened by Andrew Wilson in his review of the show as 'similar to the construction of a cosmology of the Middle Ages, a world poised between fantasy and reality but which threatens our perceptions of both'.[12] The works, and thus the viewer are trapped in a swirling mass of imagery, the constituent parts of which are not necessarily threatening or chaotic when addressed individually, but overwhelming when combined, forcing our eyes open, and forcing us to interpret the works for ourselves. As Hirst describes it, 'it's like there is a lot of energy when the aeroplane explodes and there is a lot of death after it has exploded but it is at the point where it is exploding, and I quite like it on that level'.[13] There is a huge sense of being caught in the middle of something more powerful than ourselves, of a chaotic power about to be unleashed, and we are given little or no assistance from the artists about how to handle it.

Hirst echoes earlier statements from his career when he says, 'the artists aren't actually saying something so specific and the viewer has to do a lot of work and will feel uncomfortable. If you decide on an interpretation you very much feel that it is your interpretation. The viewer should be made to feel responsible'.[14] We are buffeted with nihilistic and unsettling ideas which seem to be completely out of control. It is this sensation of chaos that fuels Hirst's own and a good deal of other contemporary art, British and otherwise. It is about 'that kind of dealing with life when things are, in a way, out of control, when there is this over-layering of meaning giving this intense activity which is like life to me, a writhing pit of snakes'.[15]

Some Went Mad ... Some Ran Away ... broke attendance records, and Hirst seems to have gained even more self-confidence from this. His latest installation, which is to raise funds for the production of an opera, is not unlike *In and Out of Love* or *Modern Medicine*, in that he has again created a sort of ecosystem. 30 rats will live for three weeks in a steel cage suspended over household ferns. A costume from the opera hangs in the cage, and music from it plays on a 12 minute loop. The lighting varies, and as it gets brighter, we realise that the rats are living amongst medical packaging. It is Hirst's hope that the rats will breed and live happily amongst the packaging. The cage is suspended over a nonspecific embryonic form, which again evokes Hirst's preoccupation with the life/death cycle. He says, 'it's all about facing the idea of death in order to move forward. You have the end of one civilisation, and the beginning of another, all juxtaposed'.[16] Most of the papers focus on the rats and the squirmy qualities of it all, but Hirst is correct in saying that he does use old-fashioned ideas in his work; like the others, this sculpture has provoked media attention and debate in quarters which are unusual for discussion of the aesthetic to take place.

Within the context of *Some Went Mad ... Some Ran Away ...* it is easily realised that Burke's system of the sublime is still, after all this time, a viable proposition. Perhaps it can be attributed to the times we live in. Damien Hirst and a few others like him have made the transition from the Thatcherite 80s to the as yet incompletely characterised 90s very smoothly. Hirst has developed into an extremely professional artist, a highly motivated developer of his own career. He took the Thatcherite message of 'On Yer Bike' to heart and made the world discover him, instead of just waiting for it to catch up. He is also seeking new avenues: his next intended project is a TV advertisement for a cable

station which is exclusively devoted to B-movies.

Hirst is now in an ideal position to challenge the ways in which we view art. By taking it out of its usual over-administered context and giving ultimate responsibility for interpretation back to the viewer where it rightly belongs, Hirst has brought a breath of new air, even if that air does at times reek of the charnel house. 'Hirst has introduced a dimension of mystery, probably with the intention of conjuring up the fragile nature of life and the randomness of social order, and has done so without falling into the irritating trap of moralisation . . . '[17] By introducing this element of mystery and chaos into his own work, and giving other artists the opportunity to do the same, Hirst has put everything up for re-negotiation, which is both invigorating and terrifying at the same time. Richard Shone's essay which introduces the catalogue for Some Went Mad . . . Some Ran Away . . . begins thus: 'An urge to bring order to chaos – the search for meaning in the seemingly random flux of experience – has existed as a fundamental human motivation throughout history . . . Works of art are one of the major sources of data in the explanation of this universal need'.[18]

This urge to impose order is, I agree a funda- mental human quality and forms the basis of literally tons of philosophical dissertation. The sensing of this chaos, and our hopelessness in the midst of it is what can cause some of our deepest fears and provoke some of our strongest emotional reactions. To many, death is chaos simply because of its unknown and unknowable qualities, and to be presented with this chaos in artistic form resounds on some of our deepest fears and results in an existential sublime exactly as Burke outlines it. Burke's theory is still valid, and will continue to be so, as long as the chaos does not swallow it up. But if it does, it will be spat out again, perhaps for another enfant terrible to address in another innovative way. Burke's theory can free us from the contemporary tendency to theorise art beyond all emotional impact because of its simplicity and more basic appeal. The quality of human life has changed a great deal since Burke wrote the Philosophical Enquiry, but it is unlikely that basic human nature and perceptual apparatus has. Burke's theory, like many other good theories, has stood the test of time, and whether he is aware of this or not, Hirst has developed an art in which this type of sublime reaction can be experienced in a variety of constructive, life-affirming and illuminating ways.

Notes

1 Andrew Wilson, 'Out of Control', Art Monthly, June 1994, pp3-9.

2 Edmund Burke Philosophical Enquiry into the Origin of our Ideas of the Sublime and Beautiful, The Scolar Press Limited, Menston, England, 1970, p50.

3 ibid, p54.

4 ibid, p257.

5 Paul Crowther, Critical Aesthetics and Postmodernism, The Clarendon Press, Oxford, 1993, p130.

6 Adrian Dannat 'Life's like this, then it stops', an interview with Damien Hirst for Flash Art, March 1993, p61.

7 ibid, p62.

8 James Hall, 'British Art Now', ARTnews, September 1993, p14.

9 Creative Camera Magazine, April/May, 1991, inside front cover.

10 op cit, Flash Art, p62.

11 op cit, Art Monthly, p7.

12 ibid, p7.

13 ibid, p7.

14 ibid, p8.

15 ibid, p9.

16 The Daily Telegraph, 15 August 1994.

17 Eric Troncy, 'London Calling: Intimacy and Chaos in Contemporary British Art', Flash Art, Summer 1992, p87.

18 Richard Shone, Exhibition Review, London, The ICA Gallery, Burlington Magazine, March 1992, pp197-198.

Sources Consulted

Cone, Michele, 'France in Review', Arts Magazine, December 1991, pp82-83.

Godfrey, Tony, 'Damien Hirst at 2-3 Woodstock Street', Art in America, December 1991, p127.

Philips, Christopher, 'Damien Hirst at the Chiat Residence', Art in America, December 1992, pp 109- 110.

Schlieker, Andrea (ed), Catalogue for Some Went Mad . . . Some Ran Away . . . exhibition at The Serpentine Gallery, London, 4 May to 5 June, 1994. Introductory essay by Richard Shone.

Damien Hirst, Ammonium Biborate, 1993, gloss household paint on canvas

SILENT VISIONS
LYOTARD ON THE SUBLIME
Renée van de Vall

The modest revival of the aesthetics of the sublime during the last decade owes much to the writings of Jean-Francois Lyotard on the postmodern condition and on the role of the artistic avant-garde. Lyotard is one of those philosophers who not only describes present-day culture in terms of an unsolvable pluralism, but who also welcomes this pluralism as a kind of liberation. Instead of the tyranny of one encompassing discourse, there is – and should be – a multitude of genres of discourse, genres that necessarily conflict with one another. This heterogeneity of genres is for Lyotard a kind of safeguard against the easy domination of one way of writing, speaking or thinking over the others. It works against the tendency of one genre to overrule all other genres – here Lyotard thinks primarily of the economic discourse – and thereby safeguards the open spaces that allow new and unthought sentences to be formulated, which in turn verbalise undetected injustices.

In this philosophy, a special place is designated to silence. Where traditionally philosophy has regarded silence as lacunae, uncharted territory that should be mapped with concepts, reasonings and conclusions, Lyotard is very reticent. He is aware of the fact that charting a philosophical white spot is often the first stage of conceptual colonisation; and that as soon as an open spot is conceptualised, it can be used and misused by the genre he mistrusts most: the instrumental, economic discourse of capitalism. So often he rather circumscribe than describe these open places when they appear in his philosophy. Silence indicates inevitable gaps in our comprehension, gaps that should be respected, rather than bridged.

The sublime is a name for one kind of gap. Auschwitz indicates another of these gaps. Both the sublime and Auschwitz form unspeakable points in discourse, disruptions in the course of our sentences, that should be respected as such. When, for instance, in the recent discussion surrounding the movie *Schindler's List*, Claude Lanzmann condemns the movie as he believes the Holocaust cannot be faithfully represented, and therefore should not be represented as Spielberg does. This argument comes close to what Lyotard would probably have to say.

I have my doubts about this philosophical position, real doubts. There is a lot to say for Lyotard's mistrust of philosophical imperialism, but on the other hand, it is my firm conviction that in his philosophy, a lot remains overlooked that is essential for the understanding and valuation of art. This will be explained by examining the experience of the sublime as it is presented in Abstract Expressionism,[1] but first more has to be said about Lyotard's reformulation of the concept of the sublime.

In Lyotard's philosophy the experience of the sublime is the experience of a discontinuity in experience, the experience of a here and now. In 'The Sublime and the Avant-Garde',[2] Lyotard takes the title of a text by the painter Barnett Newman as a starting point, 'The Sublime is Now', together with some of the titles of his sculptures and paintings, like *Here, Now, Be or Not There – Here*. He asks: 'how can one think of the sublime as a "Here" or a "Now"? Is not the sublime something beyond the here and now, beyond normal experience, something that cannot be shown or presented?'

Lyotard's answer is that the here and now, seemingly the most commonplace of experiences, is in fact the most uncommon. Nothing is as strange to us as the awareness of 'here' or 'now'. To illustrate it with the 'now', that for Lyotard seems to be more important than the 'here'. This 'now' is not a moment in time, not one in a series of events. It questions the time-sequence itself, the continuity that links one event to another. It is an awareness that locates itself outside time, space or causality. 'Who does know enough about *now*?' asks Lyotard.

Lyotard's question reminds me of a quotation I read in an essay by the American composer Morton Feldman, whose compositions stretch time unto its breaking point. Feldman quotes from *Dr Zhivago* by Boris Pasternak, who writes that in art we should confront ourselves with fear. That is difficult. Everything in our life and culture attempts to shield us from this fear. 'But there is this feeling of a danger right in front of us. And we know that this danger in front of us is neither the past nor the present, but that it is simply – the next ten minutes'.

We do not know about 'now', because we think of what is to come – of the next ten minutes – in terms of what has been. We imagine tomorrow to be a

Clyfford Still, 1957-D, no 1, 1957, oil on canvas

continuation of today. In our thinking we tame the indeterminateness of what is to come by means of expectations, plans or programmes. Intellectual and artistic disciplines and programmes presuppose this continuity. They impose it, by giving rules to link sentences to one another, rules that tell us that after this phrase there should be another, that after this colour there should be another colour. These rules encourage us to ignore the 'here' and 'now', blocking the awareness of the occurrence as such. The sublime feeling is the feeling not of what happens, but that anything happens at all. It is the old philosophical wonder that there is something rather than nothing. It indicates the eventness of the event, and as such it is outside the temporal sequence. Newman's art testifies this awareness. He does not represent sublime events, he creates them. 'Here and now there is this painting, rather than nothing, and that's what is sublime. Letting go of all grasping intelligence and of its power, disarming it, recognising that this occurrence of painting was not necessary and is scarcely forseeable, a privation in the face of 'Is it happening?', guarding the occurrence 'before' any defence, any illustration, and any commentary, guarding before being on one's guard, before 'looking' under the aegis of now, this is the rigour of the avant-garde'.[3]

The sublime is connected with terror, the fear that there will be no more happenings. Lyotard is convinced that art deprives us from this privation as it brings relief. 'Here, then is an account of the sublime feeling: a very big, very powerful object threatens to deprive the soul of any "it happens", strikes it with "astonishment" (at lower intensities the soul is seized with admiration, veneration, respect). The soul is thus dumb, immobilised, as good as dead. Art, by distancing this menace, procures a pleasure of relief, of delight . . . the soul is returned to the agitated zone between life and death, and this agitation is its health and its life. For Burke, the sublime was no longer a matter of elevation but a matter of intensification'.[4]

According to Lyotard, art in one move both stages the threat of privation, and provides the relief. The aesthetics of Burke and Kant made a negative presentation possible; they created the chance to experiment with surprising combinations. 'The artist attempts combinations allowing the event. The art-lover does not experience a simple pleasure, or derive some ethical benefit from his contact with art, but expects an intensification of his conceptual and emotional capacity, an ambivalent enjoyment'.[5]

Thereby painting had to cope with the paradox that it should testify to the indeterminate with determinate means. The modernist avant-garde responded, claims Lyotard, by questioning each and every definition of art, every rule that presented itself. Cézanne's 'petites sensations', abstraction, the disappearance of the art object in Conceptualism and Performance Art, are all seen by Lyotard as efforts of successive artists to create room to testify to the sublime, to bear witness to the indeterminate, to present the unpresentable.

This way of putting it has the advantage of acknowledging the formal renewals of the avant-garde, without depriving them of their connection with content. The Abstract Expressionists, for example, did not only do away with pictorial space or figurative elements because of a preoccupation with the medium of painting itself, but because they wanted to convey a kind of meaning they could not convey through the means they had learned. However, this close connection of the sublime with avant-garde as such, poses the question of renewal for its own sake. As Lyotard recognises, the avant-garde runs the risk of the commercialisation of the shock, the equation of the sublime with the new. The laws of the market place value renewal very highly. Is there any difference between the putting into question of the conditions of art, and the declaration that the old is old-fashioned and the new is 'in'? Lyotard is very clear on this point: the question of the sublime is something other than the shock of the new.

However, when it comes to elucidation, the way in which we make the distinction between what is sublime and what is merely new, Lyotard remains silent. Just as in Le differend, it is only because of a feeling that we know that the silence is not just a silence, but more: the silence of an injustice, or of Auschwitz, or of the sublime; as if a feeling is without articulation, form or structure, and hence cannot be elucidated. Lyotard circumscribes the silence, but does not describe what we feel and how we feel, that the silence is of one kind instead of another. For instance, even when he discusses the art of Barnett Newman, instead of concentrating on his essays or titles, he states that the paintings defy comment as well. Lyotard never describes an individual painting to explain how we, as spectators, come to feel that the sublime is now.

In Lyotard's philosophy, a painting seems to be sublime just because it is there, in spite of its doing away with traditional artistic values. It breaks the continuity of experience by depriving us of characteristics that seem to be essential for art – perspective, figuration, colour, format – and then intensifies our experience by still being there. 'Here and now there is this painting, rather than nothing and that's what is sublime.'

My objection to this is that I think that one can

intuitively recognise *many different ways* in which the unpresentable is presented and can indicate why these ways are different. This sounds paradoxical, but it is not. Even in the work of one painter (for example, Barnett Newman), the kind of experience that we roughly cover with the same name (for example, the sublime), assumes many different shades, nuances and forms.

Although they were both painted in 1951 by Newman, the paintings *Vir Heroicus Sublimis* and *Cathedra* differ greatly from one another in outlook, feeling and dynamics. We could consider both in terms of the presentation of the unpresentable, but we can also see and feel and recognise differences in how this unpresentable is presented. The same applies to the paintings of different artists that belong to the same period and break with tradition in roughly the same way. Yet how this is done and how the presentation of the unpresentable is staged might be very different in each case.[6]

It seems to me that paintings can be varied in their means and effects, although this does not imply that these means are subject to the kind of conceptual determination Lyotard attemps to avoid. What I would like to demonstrate is that paintings can indeed disrupt a certain sense of spatial or even temporal continuity, denying us well known means of orientation as Lyotard's aesthetics of the sublime would have it. This constitutes the negative stage of the sublime experience, the feeling of displeasure. However, the positive stage of the sublime experience can be articulated in a more interesting manner than that by Lyotard. At the same time that a work disrupts our feeling of spatial or temporal coherence, it can propose different forms of continuity, different logics of orientation. In a short and Kantian formulation it can stage different forms of imaginative synthesis than the form that is determined by conceptual identity. These forms are open, they do not force the spectator but invite him to identify imaginatively with a certain position in the virtual space of the painting and to look and see accordingly.[7]

As examples I shall discuss three paintings by three different Abstract Expressionist painters: Barnett Newman himself, Mark Rothko and Clyfford Still. The names of these painters are often mentioned together, because of their styles as well as their subjects. They all painted large colour-field paintings, they knew each other and more or less worked together in a short but crucial period in their careers during the late 40s in New York. Their art is often connected with the sublime, mainly because the large colour-fields evoked suggestions of the infinite.[8] Despite these strong connections, however, the sensations their paintings evoke

are quite different. Generally speaking, one could state that the three painters broke with tradition in comparable ways. All three challenged the continuity and wholeness of spatial experience, but if one examines their paintings more closely, it appears that these challenges were very different.

It is very important to consider the visual impact of these paintings. In each one a well known, objectifying organisation of space is denied to the spectator. This is because it is impossible to see the surface of the paintings unambiguously in one total overview. Furthermore, another form of spatial organisation is offered through orientation that is affective and emotional, instead of measuring the closeness or distances between the objects, and between the objects and oneself. Both the discontinuity and continuity are suggested to the viewer by the individual visual dynamics of the works.

In *1957-D, no 1*, by Clyfford Still, the continuity of the surface is challenged by the sharp, haggard forms, the irregular silhouettes and the sharp contrasts between light and dark which give an impression of utter arbitrariness. The painting is very large, about three metres high by four metres wide, but that is not all. It is too irregular and too full of visual conflicts to be endured by the eyes. One's eyes are directed in too many directions at once and the contrasts between light and dark are painful to look at. Furthermore, it is not obvious what should be seen as figure and what should be seen as ground. The large yellow, vertical form at the right-hand side could be seen as a figure, but at the same time it serves as a ground for the black forms surrounding it, or for the white spots in its middle. It is a dry and harsh painting, but this is part of its beauty. There are moments of quietness and tranquillity in it, even if temporarily. The red spots in the yellow stripe in the middle are beautiful – if you forget the rest of the painting for a moment. In the same way, one can escape in one or the other of the little islands of white, or yellow and white. As long as one tries to see the painting in its entirety, it is an attack on the eyes, but as soon as one forgets that, as soon as the eyes are free to wander from one spot to the next, then one notices the pleasure in all those spots of light. Hence, the painting can be confronted – or viewed – in two ways: either in a distanced, objectifying manner where one attempts to encompass the field of vision in one overview; or in a more playful, erratic, partial manner, where one immerses oneself in what one is faced with.[9]

Blue, Green and Brown by Mark Rothko, 1951, measuring two-and-a-half by two metres, also challenges an objective way in which to view a painting, but in a less aggressive manner. Here there are no sharp contrasts or 'weird' forms, but there are subtle tensions and hidden depths which make it impossible to see the picture as a continuous whole. The first impression is of an immense quietness and stillness, but as one continues looking, subtle movements can be seen. These movements are very complex results of the visual pressures and tensions in the painting. They change, depending on whether the upper or lower part of the painting is being examined. It is not a homogeneous painting, although the blue colour pervades all other colours and keeps the painting together. There are movements forwards, in the direction of the viewer, but also backwards, into the optical depths of the painting; as there are horizontal and vertical movements to the inside and outside of the painting. For instance, the rectangular forms in the lower part of the painting tend to broaden themselves horizontally, pushing against the left and right hand edges of the canvas. Seen along the vertical axis they hang down heavily, although because of their light horizontal edges they also remain transparent and afloat. In the blue field in the upper part of the painting the direction is kept in check by the thin blue stripe in the middle and by the surrounding frame of a slightly different blue. Yet the dominant movement is the downward movement below, against an upward movement above – this means that one's gaze is pulled apart. The painting forces the spectator to open his eyes very wide, to the kind of undirected vision one has when either daydreaming or momentarily absentminded.[10] In this wide focus the fields become broader and the depths become deeper than they were before. There is also some effect of the after image, the complementary colour one sees as one closes one's eyes, with the ultimate consequence that inside vision and outside vision tend to merge into one.

There are more ambiguities. The blue edge around the upper blue field can be seen as a kind of window sill, framing a deep space, but at the same time it can also be seen as its opposite. Hence, the blue field that was a depth now becomes a curtain, and the blue that was a frame is now a space further away.[11] The light stripes between the forms in the lower part suggest a light source that is yet further away. This ambiguity gives an impression of oscillation, of the forms and colours hovering in a continuous tension.

Just as in Still's painting, but yet in a completely different way, it is impossible to stand at a distance and view this painting as a whole. One cannot look at it without starting to lose oneself in the painting; at the same time it is impossible to dream away undisturbed, as there remain subtle frictions at the edges of one's awareness. It is both radiant and melancholic, serene and full of uncertainties. It presents a sense of space, but also of time – something is imminent, but not yet there. The objective space dissolves in a very ambivalent and emotional space.

In the same way, but again quite differently, Barnett Newman's *Vir Heroicus Sublimis*, 1950-1, confronts us with two different ways of looking, solicited by two different organisational structures, or, to be more precise, by a subtle indeterminateness in its structure which leaves us uncertain about our own stance towards what we see. Where Rothko's painting leaves us in an ambivalence and suggests an event that remains in abeyance, in Newman's painting there is something like a climax, or a resolution of the tensions it evokes.

Here, as well as in the other paintings, there is the denial of an unambiguous field of vision, the impossibility of an overview. The way in which each of the stripes ('zips' as Newman called them) is placed on the red surface makes it impossible to locate them 'in front of' or 'in between' or 'down in' the red fields. Each stripe has a different visual effect on the surrounding red colour. In some places the red field has a certain depth, as on both sides of the two light cadmium red zips; in other places it is flat, as besides the brown zip; while the flashing light of the white zip makes the red a little less red. The two light red zips stand *in* the field, the white zip *cuts through* the red, the brown zip stands *in between* the red. Therefore it is impossible to oversee the image or to view it as one single visual field. Of course the immensity of the painting adds to this impossibility, especially if we view it close up, as Newman intended us to do. But there is more to it than just the size.

Furthermore, the red hue comes towards you, especially if one no longer tries to fix the image in a constant overview. However, as this proves to be an impossible task, it is best to succumb to a more furtive, sometimes seemingly inattentive, unfocused way of looking. The red is a dense, very tactile colour, almost like a mist. The central field comes nearer than the two side panels (the painting is a triptych), but it remains restrained, as David Sylvester points out: 'it only advances towards us, it doesn't engulf us. It is immaculately flat; at the same time it becomes 3-D through its animation of the space in front of it'.[12] It is a threat kept at a distance – a classical, Burkean definition of the sublime.

The white zip cuts through this red mist. It does many things at once: by its position it makes the composition seem asymmetrical; it blinds and hurts the eyes, but as it breaks through the burning and suffocating red, it comes also as a relief; it gener-

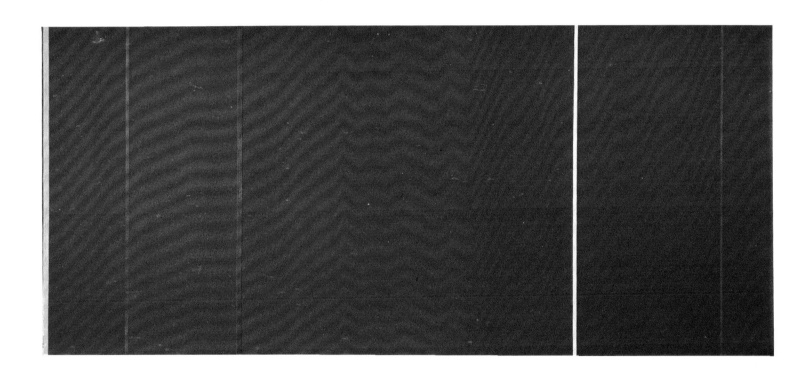

ates, as Sylvester wrote, an explosive tension, and cuts through us, but at the same time it prevents us from losing ourselves in the visual illusion of the dense, red mist. Sharp and severe as the white zip might be, it nonetheless gives us a sense of direction, of relief, of identification. The painting disorganises our vision, yet organises it. We lose our hold on it, we seem to get lost, but at the same time we recover our sense of orientation, no longer as an overview, but as an identification – as Newman called it, a sense of place.

Writing about Newman, Lyotard tells us that there is hardly anything one can say about his work, everything is present and the only thing one can add are exclamations like: 'Ah!' or 'look at that!' Expressions, he continues, of what is traditionally called the sublime.[13] I think Lyotard both underestimates Newman's work and the sublime in art. In his theory, what one could call the 'sublime turning', the passage from a feeling of pain or frustration to a feeling of delight, is more or less independent from the visual appearance of the painting itself. It is located in the way a painting is connected to its predecessors. As soon as it disappoints our experiences – yet manifests itself as a painting – it can be called sublime.

However, in the three paintings discussed above, there are less superficial reasons to speak of the sublime. Their visual dynamics engage the spectator in a contradictory experience: first of a rupture in a familiar way of orientation – one that could be called 'objectifying', then of the possibility of a different form of spatial 'organisation' – one that is guided by more affective and imaginative ways of orienting oneself in space. This is not to deny its 'otherness' or elusiveness. This different way of orientation can be felt and can even be described up to a certain extent, but it cannot be grasped and comprehended conceptually as objective experience can. Yet it can be evoked by a painting. And only by connecting the sublime to the way a painting evokes its experience, can we formulate a philosophy of the sublime that is more than a theoretical construct, elucidating for us something we really feel.

Notes

1 I have done so more extensively in my thesis, *Een subliem gevoel van plaats. Een filosofische interpretatie van het werk van Barnett Newman*, Historische Uitgeverij, Groningen, The Netherlands, 1994.

2 This text has been published in English in several volumes with articles by Lyotard. Here I quote from *The Lyotard Reader*, ed. Andrew Benjamin, Basil Blackwell, Oxford, 1989.

3 *ibid*, 'The Sublime and the Avant-garde', p199.

4 *ibid*, p205.

5 *ibid*, p206.

6 For this argument it makes no difference whether the sublime is taken in its modernist, nostalgic variety, as the lack of protestations, or as the postmodern sublime that is characterised by Lyotard as *novatio*, 'the increase of being and the jubilation which results from the invention of new rules of the game, be it pictorial, artistic or any other'. See Lyotard, 'Answering the Question: What is Postmodernism?', *Innovation/Renovation: New Perspectives on the Humanities*, eds. Ihab and Sally Hassan, The University of Wisconsin Press, 1983, pp338-341.

7 There are many art historians and philosophers that have contributed to the ideas I propose here, among them Susanne K Langer, *Feeling and Form*, Routledge and Kegan-Paul, London, 1953; Umberto Eco, *L'oeuvre ouverte*, Éditions du Seuil, Paris, 1962; Richard Wollheim, *Painting as an Art*, Princeton, NJ and London, 1987; and Paul Crowther, *The Kantian Sublime: From Morality to Art*, The Clarendon Press, Oxford, 1989.

8 See Lawrence Alloway, 'The American Sublime', *Living Arts*, Vol I; no 2, June 1963, pp11-22; Irving Sandler, *The Triumph of American Painting*, Harper & Row, New York, 1970; Robert Rosenblum, *Modern Painting and the Northern Romantic Tradition: Friedrich to Rothko*, Thames and Hudson, London, 1975.

9 Here one could usefully evoke Norman Bryson's distinction between the Gaze and the Glance; I would be very reluctant however to draw any far-going psycho-political or ideological conclusions from such distinctions. Norman Bryson, *Vision and Painting: The Logic of the Gaze*, Harvard University Press, New Haven and London, 1983.

10 For psychoanalytical descriptions of this 'wide focus' Marion Milner, *On Not Being Able to Paint*, Heinemann, London, 1950/71; and Anton Ehrenzweig, *The Hidden Order of Art: A Study in the Psychology of Artistic Imagination*, Weidenfeld and Nicholson, London, 1967. The best description however is a poetical one: it can be found in Rainer Maria Rilke's poem *Requiem für eine Freundin*, written for the painter Paula Modersohn Becker.

11 Peter Fuller notes this for another Rothko painting in *Art and Psychoanalysis*, The Hogarth Press, London, 1980/88, p222.

12 David Sylvester, 'The Ugly Duckling', *Abstract Expressionism: The Critical Developments*, ed. Michael Auping, New York, 1987, p140.

13 *op cit, The Lyotard Reader*, 'Newman: The Instant', p241.

Barnett Newman, Vir Heroicus Sublimis, *1950-51*

'RELIGION', TRANSCENDENCE, THE LIGHT AND THE DARK

THE WORK OF JO VOLLEY AND MARCUS REES ROBERTS [1]

Edward Winters

Any man who is halfway decent will think himself extremely imperfect, but a religious man thinks himself wretched.[2]

No cry of torment can be greater than the cry of one man. Or again, no *torment can be greater than what a single human being may suffer.*

A man is capable of infinite torment therefore, and so too he can stand in need of infinite help.[3]

I begin these remarks with an anecdote which gives particular flesh to the thought expressed in the two aphorisms. Some years ago, I heard of a man who belonged to an anonymous association. A melancholy, rather fine man, he had recounted the tale of his drinking. He told of his misery in a dignified, quiet, Irish brogue. He had been a Roman Catholic priest given to drinking gin. Steadily he would drink through the day, serving his Mass and going about his duties in a kind of alcoholic fog. In the evening he would retire to his room alone to cry. He would drift into sleep early on, wake every 40 minutes or so and sit on the edge of his bed. There he would pour himself gin, and then, after being comforted by its numbing effect, settle back down for a little rest. So, several times during the darkest hours he would find himself sipping and weeping. Eventually the birds would wake him while it was still dim, but creeping now into morning's early light – the shadowy moment between gloom and glimmer. Then he would kneel by the side of his bed and pray, 'Oh Dear Lord, please don't let the daytime come'.

There must be a sort of infinite agony attached to feeling responsible for *everything*. This poor man, in his way a Christ-like figure, must have felt punished every minute of every day.[4] And this perception of the world and one's place in it is born of the recognition of human frailty and of the immensity of the struggle one would have to be halfway decent. However, this recognition is itself an acknowledgement of the infinite might of nature; to acknowledge that the power of nature in its perfection lies beyond our understanding and that we, poor souls, drift like so much flotsam afloat on the foam. Our natural days are spent according to the dictates of an all powerful 'Thing'. Our skin

loses its elasticity because of what we are and because of where we dwell in the scheme of natural objects. But we alone can come to recognise this. And this recognition affords us the feeble opportunity to rail against the predetermination of our flesh. Only the rational man can come to appreciate the enormity of his desolate circumstance. Yet, as persons we are born into the moral life and can come to recognise and obey the prescriptions of reason. Herein lies our freedom and the hope for our redemption, fleeting and fragile as they are. For, as against the stubborn causal account of my animation, in coming to see myself as a self-determined agent I can rise up against my carnal proclivities and in so doing, conquer my brute nature, at least until it is all over. And the thought that one day it will all be over serves to constrain my freedom; not by inhibiting it, but by setting the conditions under which it can flourish. As a person I have it in my power to act well. The human world is a world illuminated by moral thought. It is a world in which the religious glow burns on, even in an age of profanity.

If – a quite colossal if – science were to reveal that nature is not contrived, then we would still feel the burden of the enormity that shapes us, dumb and brute this time but still beyond our grasp, and just as terrifying for that. Moral judgement is justified by reason, and so we are compelled to think of values as rational. It is reason itself that underwrites our freedom. But reason, like nature, is infinite. Nature is vast, containing, making us feel insignificant in its presence. This feeling, born of reflection, disturbs us. But that which contains us can itself be contained by us, at least in thought. In this we come upon the ambiguous consolation of calm, rational, 'religious' reflection and the feeling of the sublime that such reflection engenders.

We live nowadays in an age that mistrusts the grand narratives which held our forebears captive. It is for this reason that I feel urged to use the word 'religion' protected by inverted commas. It is perhaps because the thoughts and feelings of which I write lie beyond the scope of narrative, that one thinks in terms of vague feelings and transcendence. These promptings go beyond the particulars of *my* situation; of *this* age; of this or that theologi-

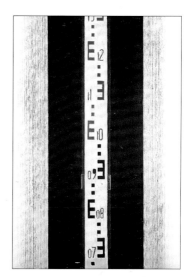

OPPOSITE: Marcus Rees Roberts, Man by a Grey Wall, *1993, oil on canvas; FROM ABOVE: Jo Volley,* The Diagonal, *1994, oil and wax on canvas; two details of Jo Volley's* Staff, *1994, oil and wax on canvas*

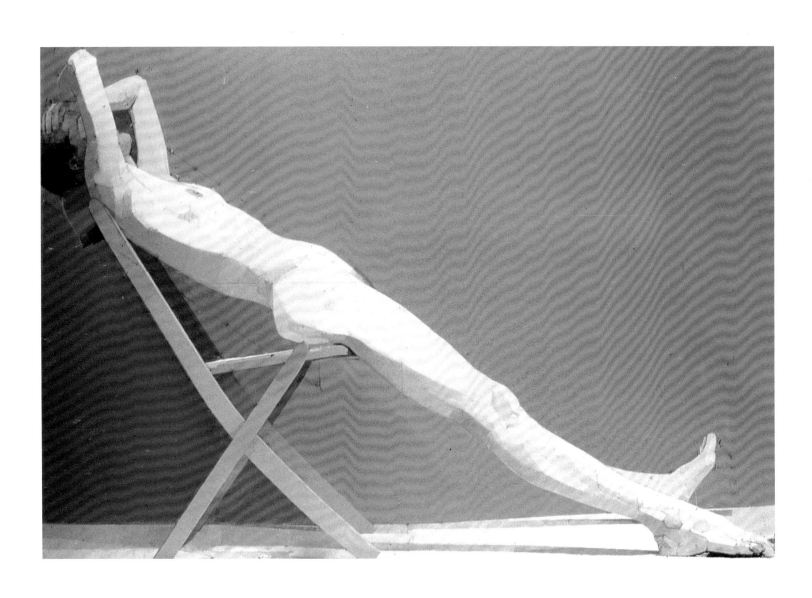

cal doctrine. They are pointers which have led us to peer into a dark fog, they intimate a realm of value which at once disturbs and comforts us, but these thoughts lie at the edge of our world where the form of our thoughts is hardly discernible. They lie beyond what can easily be measured or spoken of. If these lie at the edge of rational thought, intimated by it but barely contained within it, then perhaps they might better be revealed by art. How can these intimations of what and how we are be the subject of pictorial art?

The following sensitive, suggestive and perceptive passage by Mel Gooding gives a sense of the profundity of these paintings: 'behind the scrupulous precision and concentration of Jo Volley's painting lies an idea that has animated the work of the great painters of still life, of the static figure or of object. It is to pay this kind of attention to the object, to depict it with such fidelity, is to make another level of seeing possible, the vision of what lies behind appearance. Volley's pictures seem to be transfigured by a light that comes from within the paint itself. It is a clarity that comes from a directed intensity of focus, the only purpose of which is the discovery of the image on the canvas. Such singularity of creative intent, undistracted by any formal considerations, magically transforms ordinary objects, investing them with strangeness and beauty'.[5]

In these later works Volley uses quotidian instruments of measurement as her subjects. Her concern with measurement is an inheritance of her education at the Slade School where she worked with both William Coldstream and with Euan Uglow. Two paintings refer directly to Uglow's work, *Diagonal* and *Staff*. The latter is a life size painting of a land surveyor's staff. It refers to Uglow's *Nude, from twelve regular vertical positions from the eye*, 1967, winner in 1971 of the John Moores' Prize.[6] In the execution of his painting Uglow built a contraption to shift his eye level 12 times in order to minimise the perspectival distortion of looking up and down the figure. It is this same obsession with accurate observation of what the subject *is* that drives Volley's work. In *Staff* she paints a relatively flat object at full scale, measuring the surface of the surveyor's staff and transposing those measurements onto the painting. There is no perspectival distortion because she paints the object in elevation, in the manner of an architect's elevation drawing. That is, the perspectival *appearance* of the building is forfeited in order to arrive at some 'truer' map of what the building is like.

Uglow's *Nude* has at various vertical intervals 12 eye levels. This multiplication of eye levels serves to fragment (albeit in a structurally significant way)

the virtual position of the ideal spectator. The actual spectator, in his attempt to assume the position of his virtual ideal, must relocate his point of view as he looks up and down the canvas. Of course, the multiple point of view is familiar to us from both the cubists and those who work with collage. But what of Volley's work? Since her paintings are life size and use the convention of the architect's elevation, there is no one point of view on the painting at all. One views the surface of the painting as one would view the surface of the flat objects that she draws. No virtual position is geometrically implied and so there is no definite number of points of view onto the painting. This has a quite peculiar effect on the spectator as one finds one's gaze wandering around the painting, and is drawn to scrutinize the surface, focusing on the subtle colour modulations which represent the objects she paints. Here, we might remember Mel Gooding's phrase that things are seen in her pictures, 'as if transfigured by a light that comes from within the paint itself'.

This artistic concern with fidelity has its philosophical origins in antiquity. Plato, in *The Sophist* at 235d-236c, brings out what he considers to be a distinction between 'likeness making' and 'semblance making'. In the dialogue between the Stranger and Theaetetus, the Stranger, by asking a series of questions, gets Theaetetus to aver the distinction. The perfect example of the making of likenesses (*eikastiké*) consists in creating a copy that conforms to the proportions of the original, giving 'the proper colour to every part'. Sculptors or painters whose works are of colossal size, however, distort the proportions of the original in order to cope with perspectival distortion. 'If they were to reproduce the true proportions of a well-made figure . . . the upper parts would look too small, and the lower too large, because we see the one at a distance, the other close at hand . . . So artists, leaving the truth to take care of itself, do in fact put into the images they make, not the real proportions, but those that will appear beautiful'. The first kind of image, a likeness (*eikon*), is concerned with truth, whereas the second, semblance-making (*phantastike*) is concerned with appearances.

Plato clearly thinks of the making of semblances as a sort of deceit. It is with truth that he is concerned and this is unquestionably at the heart of Jo Volley's preoccupation with the nature of representation in her work. Her denial of perspective construction has its counterpart in her use of colour. She refuses to paint by using colour and tone to model the content of her paintings, steadfastly responding to the local colour of the object she depicts instead. In this she sets herself within

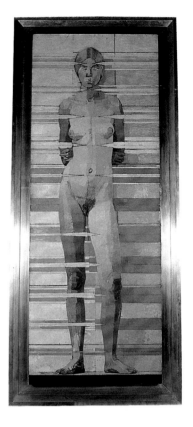

OPPOSITE: Euan Uglow, The Diagonal, *1977, oil on canvas; ABOVE: Euan Uglow,* Nude, 12 Vertical Positions, *1967, oil on canvas*

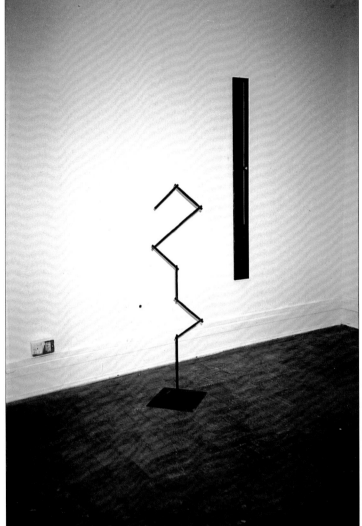

a pre-Renaissance naturalistic tradition, using colour to reveal the nature of the objects of her vision. The main concern is with the nature of light as it falls upon the surface of the object. Volley attempts to provide us with images of these instruments that 'conform to the proportions of the original' and give 'the proper colour to every part'.

(If God sees objects He will see them as they really are and not from any distance or from any angle. He will not have any particular point of view. Our concept of God, in this respect, is like that of our ideal science. He is the repository of every truth. And so His 'view' on the world is complete. There is no true description of the world as it was, as it is, or as it will be that is concealed from His knowledge. He, like reason, is located in neither time nor space. It follows from this that His 'point of view' on the world can occupy no position.)

Of course, these paintings neither present us with objects as they are in themselves nor as God would see them. No painting could. But the attempt to measure both proportion and colour in these terms suggests that we might think of our partial points of view as providing us with an indication of a realm which is far greater than ours and of which we are occasionally afforded a glimpse. There are allusions in some of the paintings to the religious art of the past. Volley uses gold leaf to create objects in the scale of icons, whose formal qualities remind us of a pre-Renaissance tradition. Her paintings are seen and understood as translucent surfaces, not transparent illusions – the light that falls on objects is the same light that falls on us.

It is the idea of measure, count and number that brings into focus the ability we have to grasp, contain and limit. But it is the very idea of the limits of measurability, of the unfathomable depths and of the incomprehensible magnitude of number that sets our thoughts toward the realm of the sublime. These ordinary instruments serve to remind us that we can and do measure the world around us and that we are lost forever in something so incommensurable that these instruments are as inconsequential and insubstantial as humanity itself. Volley is fond of quoting Graham Greene's Honorary Consul, who tells us, 'it's the measure that counts'. These pictures and the questions they raise recall another Greene story, The Heart of the Matter, in which, 'it seemed to Scobie that life was immeasurably long. Couldn't the test of a man have been carried out in fewer years? Couldn't we have committed our first major sin at seven, have ruined ourselves for love or hate at ten, have clutched at redemption on a fifteen year old deathbed?' These, I like to think, question the nature of measurement and the measure of man.

It is easy to see where these paintings belong within the Slade School tradition, but it is interesting to compare them to other artists from without that tradition. In some paintings the flatness of Volley's images makes a comparison with Jasper Johns' Flag series possible. In Johns' work, the prosaic nature of the flat image forces us to concentrate on the surface of the painting, encouraging us to wonder at the richness achieved by his use of encaustic. In Volley's work, as I have already mentioned, we attend to the delicacy of the surface and to the translucency that she is able to achieve. Richard Wollheim, in recommending Hans Hofmann's work, notes that, 'there is a right and a wrong way to achieve plasticity. The wrong way is to concentrate primarily on volume, that is, positive (or occupied) space, and try to render volume through tonal gradations, which involves the representation of light. What is wrong with this way is that it disrupts, or distracts attention away from, the picture plane. The right way, which preserves the picture plane, involves capturing simultaneously positive and negative (or occupied) space, and this is to be achieved by concentrating on plane, which is represented through colour'. Hofmann neatly contrasts the two ways: 'in nature light creates colour; in painting, colour creates light'.[7]

Volley's work, in other respects, might be likened to artists working in different media. In her painting, Two Thumb Tacks, the quietness of the picture, with its cool light glinting on the shafts of the pins, is so still and unassuming that it puts one in mind of some of the natural landscape pieces of Richard Long. The content of the painting, two thumb tacks at the edges of a dark interior void, is the source of a small, cool light. The thumb tacks are part of the everyday humble paraphernalia that never get looked at. In Long's work there is the bare trace of someone having made some small difference, a difference none would notice if it were not for our ability to recognise geometrical shapes. There is, in his work, the stillness and spiritual feeling that I have tried to reveal in these descriptions of Volley's paintings.

Marcus Rees Roberts is an artist who studied at the Slade School at the same time as Volley, but whose work belongs to a different tradition. Rees Roberts studied English at Cambridge before moving to the Slade to study film theory as a graduate student, writing his thesis on German Expressionist cinema. Whilst thus engaged he began to work on a series of etchings and subsequently took a second graduate course in the printmaking department. His etchings and paintings are sombre pictures and turn the viewer toward a different aspect of human infirmity.

OPPOSITE, FROM LEFT TO RIGHT: Jo Volley, installation shot, 1994, of Zig Zag (cast bronze surveyor's rule) and Football Italia – the green strip reflecting the one which appeared last season at the side of the TV screen to show how much of the game had passed (oil and wax on board); Jo Volley, Addition and Subtraction, 1994, oil and wax on board with gold leaf; FROM ABOVE: Jo Volley, Thumb Tacks, 1992, oil and wax on board; Jo Volley, House, 1992, oil and wax on board with gold leaf

In *The Winter Journey* series, Rees Roberts exploits his full range of skill within the medium. He uses aquatint, mezzotint, drypoint, hard and soft grounds, line, tone, sugar-lift, photo-etch, burnish and scuff. He draws, paints with stop-out varnish, uses photographic images and text, and proves his ability to use different states of the plate. This virtuosity is put in the service of his desolate view.

In a passage from *Sexual Desire*, Roger Scruton writes that we are bound to see ourselves and others as persons, as *selves* and as responsible agents, bound by the strictures of moral reason rather than by the compulsion of natural urgency. He argues that these may be no more than metaphysical shadows, shadows without which our already dreadful lives would be unbearably so.[8] These dark pages of romantic philosophy are given pictorial expression in Rees Roberts' etchings. Here, again, we find an artist who is concerned with the status of persons and with the conditions of their freedom. He uses chiaroscuro to present us with a dark world inhabited by contorted and disfigured humans engaged in the twisted and disjointed goings-on that are nightmarish exaggerations of the things we see around us everyday. A woman grown fat and wrinkled with age and misuse peers into a heart-shaped mirror to inspect her beauty, oblivious of her wretched condition. Old men have no teeth. They have dugs where they once had pectorals and these flaccid folds of flesh lap gently over great guts, but still these gentlemen wear feathers in their caps. None of Rees Roberts' characters appear to have any real purpose and yet all of them look busy. They appear in the gloom, only partially revealed or lightly defined in the darkness of the black velvety aquatints. It is a world full of shadowy incident, but divested of the metaphysical shadows of personhood and responsibility. A text appears, but is erased or obfuscated in the same way to give us a snippet of Beckett or a piece of pretentious prose culled from a piece of modern theory. The text is treated as part of the image, of the overall design of the print and it hardly seems to matter if the viewer does or does not read the surviving parts or that remain decipherable through the aquatint and burnishing. These are like conversations half remembered or perhaps only half understood, drifting like empty noise in the void. Rees Roberts' prints are as dark as his German Expressionist forebears; as bleak as grim Goya etchings and his late *Black Paintings*. They belong in the tradition that makes these comparisons possible, yet they exploit modern techniques and belong to the contemporary world.

The first print in *The Winter Journey* is a photographic image with a text etched and no apparent drawing. A later stage sees the erasure of the text with stop-painted and sugar-lift images obscuring the photographic image. This use of the different states of the plate allows Rees Roberts to employ a full range of techniques and to develop an image, demonstrating the 'painting-out' that has become a dominant feature of the visual art of this century. The photo-text title plate would not stand alone as a work of art, but becomes a work of art in virtue of its incorporation in the full series. By using the series, the artist is able to understate in some prints, making the subtlest of markings and intrusions upon the image, and then using his drafting skills to full effect in other plates within the group. By re-working the plates the series is able to degenerate chronologically with the plate. This aligns the form of the work with its pitiable content.

In the *Bluebeard* series, the image is more predominant, with small pieces of text marginalised and obscured by the sombre aquatints. The images are of a less frantic world, but it remains a dark world as if seen through a glass. This work is in a tradition: it takes and uses techniques that would not have been available to Rembrandt or Goya or the Expressionists of the 20s, yet in using these techniques he brings them into play with a repertoire which enables us to see the work as a continuation of those other artists. The art of his etching absorbs them into his picture-making in such a way that they are barely obtrusive. These pictures fall most easily into a narrative tradition and yet they seem, paradoxically, to be anti-narrative. They are pictures of people dancing and eating and waiting and wailing, but there is nothing that forms a story. In this respect the work Rees Roberts undertook as a film student shows through. His concerns with the direction of light, in both the etchings and paintings, reveals his knowledge of German cinema. However, the anti-narrative tendency, within a narrative tradition of picture-making, reveals his acquaintance with, and indebtedness to, the critical theory of Berthold Brecht. He works on the picture in such a way that questions the conventions of narrative. His texts appear but they are scuffed and partially erased, so that what appears at first glance to be a possible explanation, turns out to be disconnected, often having no relation whatsoever with the pictorial content. The pictures themselves might initially be thought to illustrate a theory, but they are in fact a shadow or an echo; a feeling rather than thoughts.

I doubt very much if Rees Roberts, in these works, shares anything of Brecht's political ambitions. That is not the point. Rather, his use of techniques and theory drawn from other etchers, painters, writers and film-makers brings a richness

Marcus Rees Roberts,
Bluebeard, *1990, etching,*
aquatint, photo-etch

to these works that is rare in contemporary work. Perhaps it is the anti-narrative strain that warns us that life, without the values we inherited from our forbearers and which we are bound to bequeath to our progeny, will come to this. It is a world in which we are divested of the dignity for which we might yet hope. And whilst it shows creatures in a hopeless condition, it shows them peculiarly illuminated from beneath, or from odd angles, dramatically lit as if in a *film noir*.

The work of Volley and Rees Roberts requires us to take in an aspect of our lives and of what we are. But each requires that we bear in mind that 'other' aspect of ourselves in order to see that what we are offered is *only* an aspect. In Volley's work we are shown a representation of the illumination of the world in which we live; and we are brought to think of the source of light and of life. Rees Roberts shows a dark world in which human creatures have no souls; a world set apart from ours. Both sets of pictures enjoin us to transcend the common world of human commerce and to consider our status as persons. These artists bring to mind the ultimate doubts, hopes and fears that we might share. Our light, like that of Volley's paintings, radiates from a different source. Our small comfort, looking into the world of Rees Roberts' pictures, comes from the thought that we inhabit a different world; a world in which we are capable of achieving dignity. Volley's paintings are more abstract, both in the thoughts they inspire and in the form they take. Rees Roberts' work is of a darker, more uncomfortable world. In both cases consolation is hard won and in both cases there is something we must first recognise. The idea of redemption first requires the acknowledgement of our condition; redemption is born of the hope that such recognition permits.

'What inclines me to believe in Christ's Resurrection? It is as though I play with the thought – if he did not rise from the dead, then he decomposed in the grave like any other man. *He is dead and decomposed*. In that case he is a teacher like any other and can no longer *help*; and once more we are orphaned and alone. So we have to content ourselves with wisdom and speculation. We are in a sort of hell where we can do nothing but dream, roofed in, as it were, and cut off from heaven. But if I am to be REALLY saved, what I need is *certainty*, not wisdom, dreams or speculation – and this certainty is faith. And faith is faith in what is needed by my *heart*, my *soul*, not my speculative intelligence. For it is my soul with its passions, as it were with its flesh and blood, that has to be saved, not my abstract mind. Perhaps we can say: Only *love* can believe the Resurrection. Or: It is *love* that believes the Resurrection. We might say: Redeeming love believes even in the Resurrection; holds fast even to the Resurrection. What combats doubt is, as it were, *redemption*.'[9]

When the Irish priest told of his life he remarked that after Vatican II, which introduced the new order of the Mass, a priest was obliged to face his congregation. This had bewildered him. Previously, his Mass had been served with his back to the congregation facing the altar, bathed in the light from above. But facing the body of the church and the darkness in which his flock was held, he had come to shake and tremble, sometimes at the point of losing control. Whichever way he turned, it must have been a dreadful test of his faith; an occasion for doubt. But the *absence* of doubt would provide no hope for redemption and would thereby preclude the possibility of faith.

Notes

1 Earlier versions of the parts of this essay concerned with the work of Jo Volley were given as 'conversations' with her at the Tate Gallery, the Chelsea Arts Club and at the Slade School of Fine Art. I am grateful to Michael Sullivan for his numerous helpful and illuminating suggestions.

2 Ludwig Wittgenstein, *Culture and Value*, Basil Blackwell, Oxford, 1980, p45e.

3 *ibid*, p45e.

4 This interpretation was suggested to me by Dan Cotterill.

5 Mel Gooding, *The Critics' Choice, New British Art*, Christies Catalogue, 23rd September 1993.

6 The John Moores' Prize was at that time the major annual prize awarded to a British painter for a painting of distinction.

7 See Richard Wollheim, 'Hans Hofmann: The Final Years', *Modern Painters*, Vol 1, no 2, Summer 1988.

8 Roger Scruton, *Sexual Desire*, Weidenfeld and Nicolson, London, 1986, p57.

9 *op cit*, Wittgenstein, p33e.

OPPOSITE: Marcus Rees Roberts, The River in the Heart, 1993, etching, aquatint, photo-etch; ABOVE: Marcus Rees Roberts, The Heart Reduced, 1989, etching, aquatint, photo-etch

THE CONTAINMENT OF MEMORY
DUCHAMP, FAHRENHOLZ, AND THE BOX
Paul Crowther

As noted at the beginning of this issue of *Art & Design* the 'sublime' has varieties, bordering on, and overlapping with, other forms of experience. The Kantian sublime, in particular, has these broader kinships, and its key structural feature can even clarify non-sublime art. At the heart of this is the question of to what degree a work gravitates around a relation between, in the most general terms, *containment and excess*. The excess, and the mode of its containment can be characterised in many different ways. In this essay I shall focus on the way in which even so modest a sub-tradition as the box can involve such a relation as a central feature. To show this, I shall first make some general points about the link between art, constants in perception and the structure of art-historical change. On the basis of this, I will consider the genesis of the box as a distinctive artistic format – with special reference to the *Green Box* and *Travelling Box* by Duchamp. One of the important themes considered in this context will be the relation between containment and memory. I shall then develop this further through an analysis of a contemporary artist Mateusz Fahrenholz.

I

The traditional media of painting and sculpture link up in many complex ways with constants in human experience. Painting, for example, plays substantially on the relation of figure and ground (a relation which characterises abstract tendencies as much as representational ones). The potency of figure/ground derives in turn from that foreground/background relation which characterises perception itself. This relation is not just a visual one. For it overlaps further with notions of proximity and distance, and is determined fundamentally by the fact that an embodied subject's hold on the world is a limited one. The experience of such a subject is constituted by the shifting relation between that which is immediately accessible to sensori-motor exploration and that which is not.

These considerations are also linked to another characteristic of the painting, namely its having an edge or limit. The edge demarcates an area of the visual field as a candidate for close attention. But more than this, the circumscription defines those qualities of interrelation which holds between the items in it. Again, in perception itself, the area which becomes the foreground of a subject's attention, and the nature of its relation to the background, are not just matters of physical positioning. The content and structure of these relations are circumscribed and given their particular character by the nature of the particular interests and aptitudes of the individual embodied subject. A painting (in terms of its status as a virtual or quasi-virtual space) internalises and declares these factors. For it does not (even in the most aggressively realist idioms) simply represent. Rather, it projects a scene or configuration, the very fabric of whose particularity determined by the artist's choices in the process of making. His or her interests, proclivities, idiosyncrasies, skills (or lack of them) and ideology are all part of the causal nexus which gives rise to the work. They are implicated in the final product – the achieved painting under the catch-all term 'style'.

Similar considerations hold in relation to sculpture. Perhaps the major difference is one of emphasis. In the transition from relief to freestanding sculpture, for example, the mobility of the foreground/background – proximity/distance relation – is accentuated simply insofar as the viewer can position him or herself in relation to the sculpture, with much greater freedom of choice.

Throughout history, painting and sculpture have always been produced with a view to specific functional ends, generally of a ritualistic or didactic kind. In most cultures these ends have been paramount, with the dimension of style relevant only in terms of skill and technical competence. However, in some cultures this normal function has been transformed by specific circumstances bound up with complex geographical, social, political and economic factors. The Italian Renaissance, for example, was an epoch when painting and sculpture began to transcend nominal religious and civic uses. Difference of vision and the individuality of style are given their due in the diversity of critical terms (using 'critical' loosely) which are brought to bear on the arts. They are seen as paradigms of rational and quasi-scientific activity, rather than achievements of craft and skill *per se*.

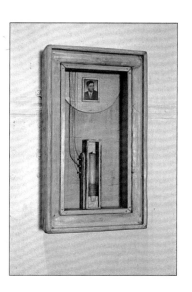

OPPOSITE: Mateusz Fahrenholz, Mother, 1991, mixed media; FROM ABOVE: Mateusz Fahrenholz, Union, 1990, mixed media; Mateusz Fahrenholz, Uncertainty, 1991, mixed media

88

This paradigm shift constitutes an orientation towards the dimension where art media exemplify constants in experience. Simple iconographic elements are now just one element in a broader fabric of meaning where emphasis falls on *how* space is generated and articulated; and on the broader symbolic associations of this. Those links with constants in experience (noted earlier) were always part of, as it were, the unconscious of painting and sculpture. Now they become more thematic elements at the iconological level.

The major legacy of the Renaissance was to establish a tradition which (like all traditions) can be analysed in two directions. The first is that of *normal historical difference*. This consists of the repetition or refinement of formats, stylistic idioms and iconographic strategies, forming the bulk of artistic production in a given tradition. Much of it involves one work differing from the other in only limited respects, such as minor stylistic inflections, or choices of subject-matter which simply reflect a broader fashion, or the institutions, or topography of a specific locale. There are, of course, gradations of such difference. One might, for example, regard the Carracci as significantly refining some achievements of the High Renaissance and Mannerism, rather than opening out radically new possibilities. On the other hand a figure such as Caravaggio institutes a moment of *effective historical difference* through the radical approach to the naturalistic and narrative function of light and other pictorial factors. He thus becomes the exemplar of a tendency leading to a distinctive new direction within tradition. Such innovations, of course, then became the conventional way to work, a focus for normal historical difference.

Under specific circumstances nowadays, a moment of effective historical difference can be so innovative as to totally transform tradition. One major example of this is the context arising from the ramifications of Picasso's *Les Demoiselles d'Avignon*, and Duchamp's unassisted ready-mades. On the basis of these a paradigm shift occurs. It involves not only the construction of alternative semantic codes to conventional pictorial representation, but also the possibility that the 'object' can be made by someone other than the artist.

The general theoretical consequences of these factors are enormous, but their ramifications can be traced in more specific directions. One such direction is the emergence of the box, as a distinctive format in 20th-century art, to which I now turn.

II

In the tritest sense, a box is for containing and/or securing and transporting things. The ubiquity of these practical functions is one reason why the box was not established earlier as a distinctive art format. Another reason is that as a bearer of surfaces – both inner and outer – the box lends itself to colonisation by painting and sculpture in terms of ornamental or representational embellishment. On these terms, whilst painters or sculptors might – as part of their general workshop practice – make the occasional decorative box, boxmaking itself remains a craft-based practice. It can be done with cleverness and massive ingenuity, but only becomes artistic to the degree that it is colonised by established art media.

Or, at least, this is how it was before the 20th century. Why, then, should matters change? There are a number of answers to this. The first is that even so modest a format as the box can draw on the same broad level of constants in experience as those noted in relation to painting and sculpture in the first part of this essay. Interestingly the most fundamental of these constants is one that does not apply to painting and sculpture with the same directness. For (even if it is not entirely covered by a lid) a box must have an inside and an outside. And in this, it partially exemplifies a relation which is definitive of human experience, namely that of *subject and object*. As subjects, our attentiveness to the present is shaped by what we can recall in memory, or what we can project in imagination. However *qua embodied* subjects, we are also situated in an objective order of material things, events and embodied subjects other than ourselves. The subject of experience is, at the very same time, an object of experience for others. Put at its crudest, we regard our bodies as 'out there', as part of the objective order, whilst our personality or subjectivity is 'in here' – it is what our body 'contains'.

Now, of course, the relationship between subject and object of experience is, in philosophical terms, enormously complex. Certainly the idea of the self being 'contained' by the body is very problematic, and, at best, would require a *great* deal of qualification in order to be accepted. Yet it is also an idea that is forced upon us by the vicissitudes of practical existence itself. For if we did not simplify the subject/object relation in terms of the inside/outside pairing, it is difficult to conceive (given the complexity and ephemerality of an animal's positioning in relation to the world) how the flux of brute consciousness might be stabilised so as to become the rational consciousness of a self. Indeed, such things as the very capacity to make shelters or boxes may themselves be implicated to some degree in the growth of such self-consciousness.

There is also a secondary level of constants to

Mateusz Fahrenholz, Elements, *1991, mixed media*

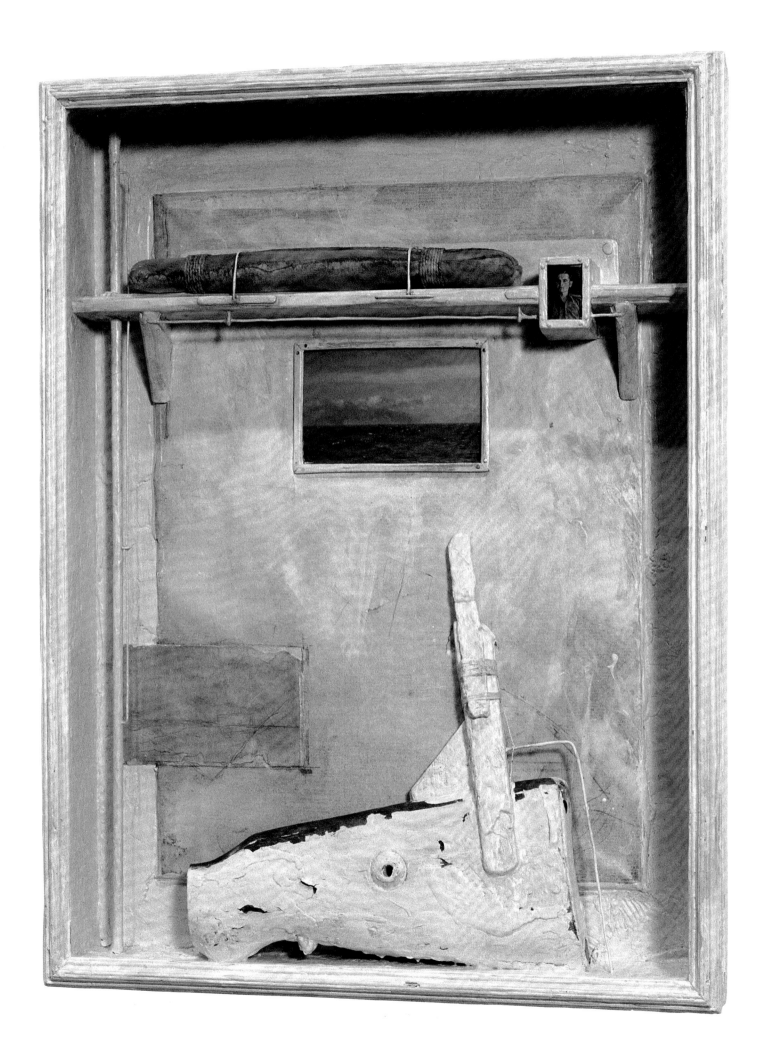

which the box might be linked. These are in the first instance of a behavioural or anthropological kind. For example, the need to contain, secure and transport things are themselves recurrent elements in the way human beings in all cultures organise their experience. And these practical functions are implicated in deeper psychological and physical needs, bound up with security and the ability to adopt to changes of circumstances. The box is an artefact with a high degree of actual and symbolic potency. For it can thematise the practical functions of containing, securing and transporting contents and thence the broader psychological and physical needs which these functions serve.

Earlier on in my discussion of painting and sculpture I suggested that the Renaissance embodied a paradigm shift. Intercourse with such media is not confined to their religious and social functions or quality of workmanship. Rather it begins to play more on a work's connection to constants in experience. It is here that we find the genesis of that tradition which, in the 18th century was finally recognised as one with its own distinctive concepts and criteria as the realm of fine art. Given this, one would expect that the box would begin to figure in the fine art tradition, when cultural conditions allowed its symbolic dimensions to emerge from the matrix of practical and decorative functions. These conditions arose with the other great paradigm shift noted earlier, namely the one instituted by Picasso and Duchamp.

Duchamp is the more immediately relevant figure. His first *Box* (this is the actual title of the work) was made in 1914. It is a Kodak photograph holder containing photographs of a drawing and 16 manuscript notes. His next venture in this direction was altogether more significant – the *Green Box* of 1934. This work (produced in a edition of 300) is composed of a suede-covered cardboard box containing fascimiles of notes and drawings involved in the creation of *The Bride Stripped Bare By Her Bachelors, Even*, 1915-23. (I shall hereafter refer to this latter work as the *Large Glass*.) Now whilst in this box the contents are derived from original works or manuscripts by Duchamp himself, they *are* fascimiles and not originals. Indeed the box itself (as in the 1914 work) is not one which the artist physically made. These works, in other words, are important elements in a broader context defined by Duchamp's 'unassisted ready-mades' ie these objects 'found', rather than made, by the artist, which are offered up, nevertheless as works (or elements within works) *by* him.

To function in this context means that interest is entirely shifted from any question of craft and skill. Attention is rather focused on the broader implica-

tions of the specific relation between the container and its contents, and in both the examples from Duchamp which we have been considering, the contents are derived from specific moments in the artist's own creative life. The box functions symbolically as a container of the self. It is important to note the multiple significance of this in relation to the *Green Box*. On the one hand, the box is a visible 'body' which contains the history of a self, ie elements of memory; on the other hand, its contents have a quite specific character. They are constituted by records of moments in the creative process (those choices and decisions exemplified in notes and drawings) which were eventually to result in a specific work – the *Large Glass*. The point is that in containing these, the *Green Box* signifies the way in which a specific made product such as the *Large Glass* only comes to be through the accumulation of moments. All these moments are, as it were, invisibly inscribed *inside* the end product. They make it what it is, even though it is not reducible to the sum of its constitutive moments or stages, nor they to it. A further aspect to this is that as well as the overt reasons for, or causal route to, any particular action or event, there are always subconscious and accidental factors involved, as well as unforeseen circumstances arising. Hence, the *Green Box* in its specific character as a specific container contrived at a specific date, is also a secondary outcome of the moments in an entirely different project – the *Large Glass*. It is thus a good example of an elusive lateral causality which operates largely unnoticed in ordinary life.

Duchamp's next major exercise in this idiom – the *Travelling Box* of 1936-1941, deepens these connections to constants in experience. It consists of a cloth-covered cardboard box containing a variety of reproductions of his works in different materials. The centrepiece of the box is a reproduction of the *Large Glass* on a sheet of transparent cellophane, set in a wooden frame. The frame is glued in place so as to stand erect when the box is opened. Other largish colour reproductions are slotted in behind the glass, and can slide out in the 'open position'. Other smaller items are also fixed in place, but the bulk of material in the box consists of loose photographs mounted on black paper.

Now in one sense, the *Travelling Box* links directly to areas already considered. It is a body which contains Duchamp's great artistic moments, but it is selective. It does not contain everything, and in this it matches the actual operations of memory, which, in a finite being, involves at best the retrieval of episodic events or series of events rather than wholesale replay. This parallel can also

Mateusz Fahrenholz, Horizon, *1991, mixed media*

be developed in more specific terms. For whilst most human beings at various points in life reappraise the pattern of their experience, there are always some events which stand out as decisive in any interpretative context. They are inescapable for us. Other events in contrast are sometimes remembered, sometimes forgotten, sometimes related to one event, and sometimes related to others. Memory, in other words, gravitates around elements of both fixity and variability. *The Travelling Box* exemplifies this structure, through the inescability of its fixed elements, notably the *Large Glass* reproduction, and the randomness of order in terms of which the other elements are arranged.

All these factors are tellingly mediated by the specific historical circumstances surrounding the creation of the *Travelling Box*. Work commenced in 1936 at a time of sustained political crisis in Europe due to the rise of Nazism. It continued through the outbreak of war, the invasion of France, and Duchamp's escape to New York. In relation to this period of creation we must always bear in mind that the ultimate outcome of these events was *wholly* undetermined at that time. Given this, it is difficult to escape the conclusion that, for Duchamp, the *Travelling Box* is at once a strategy of intellectual self-understanding and self-preservation. It involves a selective assessment of 'work to date', which through its transportable character can be carried to safety, if need be. In this way, the anthropological constants of the box (containment, security and transportability) are mediated by specific historical and individual circumstances so as to become emblematic. The box is a modest player in patterns of upheaval and loss. Through its containment of significant items, the threatened or uprooted individual can maintain some meagre continuity between the future, the present and what has gone – *no matter what*. Duchamp's *Travelling Box*, is perhaps the most complete revelation of this general possibility.

One further aspect must be mentioned. Earlier on, it was noted how key elements in the *Travelling Box* are actually fixed in place. Open it, and you see the *Large Glass*. Other images can be slid out, so that in its most complete open position, the arrangement resembles an altarpiece. Now when a box is so clearly adapted to a viewer on the basis of formats which suggest other media (and one might cite here theatre as well as painting and sculpture) it begins to draw on constants associated with those media. This is a kind of consecration of its artistic status. The elements of meaning which are most characteristic of the box not only exist alongside, but indeed here *blend in* with aspects of other media. One might say, that in the

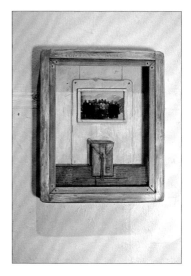

Green Box and *Travelling Box*, the box is established as art on the basis of its own distinctive criteria; and that in the latter these are also related to the broader mainstream of artistic tradition. In this way Duchamp's boxes are manifestations of effective historical difference. They inaugurate a significant new format within the radical tradition of Modernism brought about by the Picasso/Duchamp paradigm shift.

Another such moment of effective historical difference can be linked to the early works of Joseph Cornell. Before him, numerous Surrealists had worked with boxes as vehicles for personal fantasy, but Cornell refined this tendency with such obsessiveness and system, as to establish it as a familiar *way* of doing things. Duchamp's works have (as we have seen) important personal ramifications, but these are expressed in a somewhat cool, cerebral way. Cornell, in contrast, brings out the full possibility of the personal dimension. It is of the essence of a 'found' object, to be found by someone, and in Cornell's work the meaning of such an object is assigned decisively to its relation with other such items and ephemera and, more importantly, the context of finding. These factors, of course, are themselves determined by the artist's personal history and existential environments.

Now I do not propose to analyse the subsequent development of the box format in terms of its 'great' moments. A rather more interesting question is that of its minor moments. There is a banal aspect to this. The normal historical difference which constitutes the bulk of works in a tradition or sub-tradition, is just what the ingredients in the term suggest. It consists of works different from preceding works but not in any distinctive or suggestive way. They are simply 'normal'. There are, however, interesting gradations of this. For example, one would not describe a tradition or sub-tradition as healthy, unless some of its more normal works went beyond mere repetition. One surely demands that an artist who draws on idioms and ideas already laid down should do so in a searching manner. We may not learn much that is new *vis-a-vis* the further developmental possibilities of the medium, but we may learn something new about the potential of the existing idioms and ideas. This indeed is arguably just as vital to the life blood of tradition, as the moments of effective historical difference. To focus on it offers a timely corrective to the view that authentic creativity simply consists in doing something totally new (a notion which I have refuted at length elsewhere).

As an example of normal historical difference in its most positive sense, I shall address (in detail) the work of an artist still 'in the making' – Mateusz

FROM ABOVE: Mateusz Fahrenholz, Plan, *1991, mixed media; Mateusz Fahrenholz,* Partisans, *1991, mixed media*

Fahrenholz. His work is of particular interest for my present purposes in so far as it draws and develops on a number of the most important themes already explored in relation to the box format.

III

In the late 1980s the major impetus of Fahrenholz's work was towards multimedia constructions in a box-like format. These works drew substantially on images and material alluding to the sea, and owe a clear debt to the beachcomber aesthetic of Will Maclean, and (to a lesser extent) the arcane constructions of Joseph Cornell. There was, however, a crucial theme in Fahrenholz's work at this time which went beyond these precedents. His parents were Polish exiles and he himself (whilst being brought up in Scotland) was steeped in the language and ethos of Polish culture.

This personal context and its ramifications are now the major creative forces in Fahrenholz's work. In the rest of this discussion I will trace their specific manifestations, and will also consider some of their broader artistic and philosophical implications.

First some remarks upon the types and range of material employed by Fahrenholz. Many of his box-structures have the appearance of being constructed from old or 'found' material. All, however, is not as it seems. Fahrenholz paints, or treats his surfaces with wood-dye of various densities in order to give the *appearance* of being old. Wood-dye is also used to 'age' the contemporary Polish newsprint which forms a recurrent element in the box-structures. Other recurrent features include candles (as a symbol of latent energy and light), wires (as a symbol of lines of communications) and a whole range of items with domestic associations – such as bread or milk bottles. These items do not occur 'neat'. The candles have been steeped in saltwater, the bread has been dried out, and the milk bottles have been wrapped. This strategy of ostensible preservation has more complex ramifications: for again it gives the appearance of having aged; and further signifies that no matter how mundane an item is, turns of personal and historical circumstance can render it precious and thence *worthy* of preservation.

We thus arrive at the key structural element in Fahrenholz's box-structures, namely his use of old photographs. It is customary to regard photographs as the preservatory medium *par excellence*. Fahrenholz, however, interprets this in complex ways. His experience of old family snapshots has brought home to him the distance which can exist between the viewer and the persons in a photograph. No matter how much one is told about

the persons, the photograph also declares how much one does not – and if the persons are dead – cannot know. This element of abstractness – or better, indeterminacy – in even family photographs, enables Fahrenholz to feel at ease in using those images of unknown persons and places which form the bulk of his photographic material. His relation to this material, however, is not entirely indeterminate; for he has obtained much of it from Polish or Eastern European sources, a fact which is clearly reflected in the content of images.

Despite his reservations about the significance of photography, Fahrenholz accepts that it provides the 'realist' dimension through which most viewers will approach his work. Accordingly he uses specific photographs as both compositional and interpretative centres about which his associational narratives constellate. Let me illustrate this by reference to specific works.

The first is one of the most economical of his box-structures, namely *Union*. Here, the two major features are a photograph of a Polish church (in the upper zone) and a piece of bread nestling on the lower edge. This is, of course, not an arbitrary conjunction in any sense. Most obviously, the viewer is invited to make the association between church and bread in terms of the rite of the holy sacrament. But there are deeper associations still. The centrality of the Church in defining Poland's national identity is well known. Hence, just as bread is a staple of physical need, so too is the Church a staple of spiritual need and Polish nationhood. (The very title *Union* suggests the *intimacy* of this relation.)

Another of the simpler works is *Passage*. Again the upper zone of the physically shallow box-structures is dominated by a single photograph – of the old Polish liner *Batory*. The image is set at an angle, as though sailing away from the viewer into the back of the box. In the lower zone is a section of Polish newsprint with a framed portion of an old passport. Thus, in conjunction, the elements suggest a passage away from the homeland into the unknown. At the heart of this alienation is the crossing of the ocean – a motif which is found in many of Fahrenholz's works.

One of the other dominant motifs in the box structures is that of war. This theme is present as both harbinger and agent of loss and dispersal. It is, however, manifest primarily by allusion in terms of its artefacts and effects. In a work such as *Partisans*, for example, the central image of three partisan fighters from the Lwów region is defined by an uncompromising surround of black. The lower zone contains a locked and wired down casket that at once connotes ammunition-box,

FROM ABOVE: Mateusz Fahrenholz, Empire, *1991, mixed media; Mateusz Fahrenholz,* Brat, *1991, mixed media*

93

coffin, or baggage roped down on the decks of a ship. Whatever one's reading, there is an overriding sense that the ultimate destinies of the lives alluded to in this work, are *unknown*.

The effects of war receive perhaps their most poignant testimony in *Empire* and *Brat*. In the former work we find a framed portrait of an unknown Polish soldier. The soldier's expression is one of disorientation. In the lower zone, a wooden model of the Empire State building sits alongside a transformer unit. The two zones relate as an image of the psychology of exile. The glamour and dynamism of the USA cannot compensate for the loss of the homeland. This point is also made with a tangible degree of black humour in *Brat*. Here the work is organised in three sections. The upper one contains a striking photograph sent by a Polish exile in the USA to his *brat* (ie 'brother' in Polish). In the photograph, the exile stares with palpable unease at his own young American-born son (ie 'brat' in the colloquial sense resplendent in cowboy outfit and toting six-guns. The son not only embodies an alien culture, but (in this image at least) is also celebrating that very power of the gun which is so deeply implicated in the ultimate causes of his father's exile. Beneath this affecting image is a parcel buried in earth, and beneath that a portrait of an unknown man set deep beneath varnished glass. We thus move in sequence from exile, to yearning, to the waning of memory.

Each of Fahrenholz's box-structures, hence delineates by associational means patterns of exile, loss and memory in relation to particular lives. It might, of course, be thought that the specifically Polish dimension of these lives gives the works a rather narrow orientation. This, however, is not the case. For one thing the Polish experience itself has become, through the centuries, a living and potent symbol of suffering, displacement and dispersal. Even if one did not know the specifically Polish orientation of Fahrenholz's works, they would still be intelligible in terms of our broader cultural stock of knowledge and values. This raises complex interpretative issues which I shall now explore.

A first point to note is that all Fahrenholz's material has a recognisable general character. We can see at a glance that the photographs are old; that they are of, say, soldiers – and foreign ones at that. Again the recurrence of a motif such as the sea is one which draws on familiar symbolic connotations of distance and displacement, danger and passage. In other words, if one takes the trouble to look and think, Fahrenholz's imagery and the associations which they make are readily intelligible. Exile and its consequences are universal possibilities in the human condition.

What is most distinctive about Fahrenholz's works, however, is their capacity to draw on and declare something which is not readily accessible to conscious understanding, namely *the structure and function of memory itself*.

Aspects of this have, of course, already been noted earlier in relation to Duchamp. Fahrenholz, however, adopts very different artistic means which focus much more on a negative relation *between* personally and publicly significant imagery. The upshot is both an overlap with, and difference from Duchamp, in the way memory is articulated. The specific implications of Fahrenholz's position are as follows. Our common-sense notion of memory is a naive one. We imagine it to be a kind of retrieval facility which sorts through well-defined sedimented images of the past and sets them out for present attention. However, memory is actually *much* more opaque than this. What one recalls is framed and given contours by the interests of the present. But even then the content of memory is not exact, except in the most schematic sense. Fahrenholz's work, however, tacitly articulates the real structure of memory. His emphatic framing devices are emblems of present experience, the desire to fix and articulate both his own personal context and that of the unknown individuals addressed in his work. But the content which his frames contain is loose and allusive. Like the meanings of facts in any personal history, they can be read according to varying perspectives defined by one's present interests and situation. In striving to comprehend a culture and history to which he belongs, but with which he can never be wholly congruent, Fahrenholz again echoes our general relation to the material of memory. Our personal past is always to some degree alien, by virtue of the fact that it will never return. Hence, in looking back at the past on the basis of the present, we do not simply interpret it, we try to find a meaning, a redemptive narrative, a life-story, over and above mere chronological succession.

In this way we *overcome* the alien quality of our past experience and (in a sense) *the exile from ourselves* which it involves. Fahrenholz's work achieves such redemptive narratives. This is not just a case of him providing stories which give meaning to the individual lives addressed in his work. Rather he shows a way in which art itself is a tangible means of overcoming exile from aspects of one's own experience.

I am arguing then, that Fahrenholz's box-structures intuitively grasp both the indeterminacy of memory, and its striving for narrative meaning. Other artists have explored this general area in recent years. Anselm Kiefer, for example, has expressed the catastrophic dimensions of German experience in a succession of massive paintings and multimedia works produced throughout the 1970s and 80s. Nearer home, numerous feminist artists (such as Mary Kelly) have attempted to document female experience at the point where it begins to congeal into the past. These are all ambitious projects. Fahrenholz's work is much more modest in both its aspirations and means of realisation. *Yet this is precisely its strength.* Kiefer's Wagnerian excesses sometimes strike one as celebrations of those very forces of destruction which they are meant to indict. The Feminist critical works seem too often to be theoretical polemics, rather than attempts to genuinely comprehend experience through art. Fahrenholz in contrast explores themes of suffering and dislocation at precisely the

level at which such things *really* matter, namely the personal. This exploration is no mere exercise in theory. It issues in works of sombre, faded beauty which refract and redeem the individual's relation to the past. Fahrenholz's vision, in other words, is aesthetically and philosophically *authentic*.

To be authentic in these terms does not necessarily involve radical transformations of the box format. Rather, as we have seen, Fahrenholz follows precedents in relation to formal structure, and the theme of memory, which had already been broadly established by Duchamp and others. However he is able to develop these precedents in his own distinctive and illuminating way. His work is hence an example of normal historical difference in its positive mode.

Mateusz Fahrenholz, Labour, *1991, mixed media; OVERLEAF: Mateusz Fahrenholz,* Exile Radio, *1989, mixed media*